Collision Contents

Your Real Goal

by Johnny Scott

We all want to see life change in teens. Many jr. high youth ministries have discovered the importance of assimilating caring adults into the program who value doing life with adolescents. These ministries have also adopted some form of small group meeting time as a part of their larger vision for ministering to jr. highers. Almost everyone agrees that this small group interaction time can be effective. But after being inundated with the vast amount of curriculum and tools for small group leaders, have you ever found yourself back to square one, asking the question of what to do with jr. high small groups?

The answer is in defining what a great small group meeting looks like. In other words, identify the goal and communicate it to the teens in a way that resonates with them.

Without a new way of defining and communicating the wins during every small group session, many leaders feel like they've failed. Teens get frustrated just like we do, and they pick up on our disappointment with small group time. Some leaders have unrealistic expectations of jr. highers. But the fact is that many teens are not capable of articulating what God is doing in their hearts and minds. Many of these small group experiences are seeds that may not be seen for years. We want adolescents to have that breakthrough.

The act of processing faith issues in an environment with caring adults is a pathway we want to familiarize teens with. This in itself is a major win for a small group. Jr. highers are like wet cement. Very quickly they will be set in their ways. How awesome it is when teens begin to process their thoughts about faith and life in the context of a church small group! That's the payoff, and it can happen!

Constantly redefine the win! Question what you do now, and don't be afraid to experiment with redefining your jr. high small group wins. Here are some win-defining ideas from what others are doing:

* Define the win as one kid finally accepting the hug you have been offering for months.
* Define the win as kids not wanting to leave as soon as the official time is over.
* Define the win as someone remembering *anything* from last week.
* Define the win as pairing caring adults with teens.
* Define the win as trusting the Holy Spirit that more is getting through than meets the eye.
* Define the win as jr. highers simply coming back for more.
* Define the win as knowing adolescents feel loved and not manipulated.
* Define the win as adults being determined to look teens in the eye and simply listen as long as they need to talk. (If you did this at small group, it was a huge win!)
* Define the win as anything that shows you are building a relational bridge with a jr. higher!

Has a kid told you about an event happening in his life this week? It wasn't just conversation. Read between the lines. Are your teens anxious, do they want you to attend their events but don't know how to ask?

Unless they are being forced to attend small group by their parents, jr. highers do have other options. If they decided to come on their own to small group, that's a win.

Did a parent help bring them? That is a win because they feel strongly enough about their involvement to invest the time, gas, and hassle of dropping their teens off and picking them up. That is a huge win you needn't overlook. Did you get the chance to connect with that parent and say thanks? That is a bridge.

Did you get to appropriately touch every kid and say something below the surface level about who they are in God's eyes? If that is *all* you did, the whole evening was a hit! That doesn't happen at school and maybe not even at home.

Did someone bring a friend? That is a big deal if they trust you enough to let you in on their world with their friends.

Did someone express any thought that occurred to them during the week concerning last week's content? That is a huge win, and you must celebrate it. Encourage and praise any teen's attempt to take their faith into other parts of their lives.

For more great strategies, tips, and encouragement,
check out Johnny Scott's *Redefining the Win for Jr. High Small Groups,*
available from Standard Publishing (ISBN 978-0-7847-2320-3).

Before You Begin

Set list

We've broken each session of this Small Group Collision into sections that can be easily taken apart or rearranged so that you only use the elements and the order that works for your kids and their attention span, maturity, etc.

Collision elements

* **txt a frnd**—teens respond to an icebreaker question by texting each other
* **mic check**—teens play a game or do an activity based on the study's theme
* **solo**—teens read and reflect on Scripture for 5 minutes to prep for the study instead of doing homework before they arrive
* **freestyle**—teens share their reaction to the Scripture or topic by talking or texting
* **strike a chord**—teens study key Scriptures as a group and get into deeper discussion
* **encore**—leader emphasizes key points of the study
* **backstage pass**—teens communicate directly with God through worship, prayer, or contemplation
* **hit the road**—leader wraps up with a focus on life application
* **5 for 5 world tour**—5-minute challenges that teens will do for 5 days each week to put into action what you studied in small group; the leader can send these challenges via text message/e-mail/Facebook/Twitter or print the challenges as a handout from the CD-ROM and send it home with kids

Additional info for the leader

* **hidden track**—helpful tips for the leader about specific activities
* **b4 u meet**—a reminder to send teens before the small group meeting time
* **txt it**—an option in several places during the session allowing teens to text their answers to discussion questions instead of only responding out loud
* **playlist**—songs you may choose to use during your session to relate to the theme
* **aftr u meet**—an encouragement note to send teens after the small group meeting time

Using technology in your small group collision

Text time in the session

Jr. highers love texting. But we don't want them to become distracted by it. So we've come up with a few places in each session where you can allow teens to pull out their cell phones and text the answers to discussion questions to you or to their friends there in small group. Then you can ask them to put their phones away for the remainder of the time. These options allow teens to speak in their communication style within the framework of the small group structure without driving you crazy, we hope! You may choose to use this each session or on occasion.

Music to set the mood

Each session has a playlist of songs that focus on the theme of the study. You may want to download one or more of the songs (or use others you like) to play before, after, or during specific portions of the small group session.

Facebook, Twitter, MySpace

You might want to create your own group on Facebook or start your own Twitter following where all of your jr. highers can join and discuss small group topics during the week. Here you can send reminders to your teens about upcoming sessions and post the **5 for 5 world tour** items (see description on previous page). You could also send these via MySpace, text message, or old school e-mail! :)

The Messiah as High Priest

‾The Prep ‾

goal: Jr. highers will recognize the ultimate solution to our biggest problem of sin through Jesus, the High Priest.

Scriptures:
Leviticus 5:5-10; Leviticus 16:5, 15-17, 20-22; Hebrews 9:11-15; Hebrews 13:20, 21

You'll need:

* Bibles
* Pens or pencils
* A color printout or inexpensive poster of a famous work of art
* 1 black marker
* Scissors
* A square of roll paper or a poster board
* 1 or 2 paintbrushes
* Red paint (several shades, if you'd like)
* Newspapers or a tarp or something else to put under the painting area

Download and print:

* "It's a Party!" handout (1 copy, cut apart)
* **solo/strike a chord** discussion guide (1 per teen)

Optional supplies:

✦ For **backstage pass:** iPod or CD player and CD with recommended **playlist** music.
✦ For **hit the road:** Download and print copies of this week's **5 for 5 world tour** take-home page (1 per teen) if you are unable to use the technology options.

Setting it up:

✦ For **mic check**: Print off and cut apart the handout "It's a Party!" and recruit a few volunteer actors.
✦ For **freestyle**: Have the printout or poster ready of the famous work of art and the black marker.
✦ For **backstage pass**: Spread out canvas or newspaper on the floor, place the paper or poster on top, and set out the paintbrushes and different shades of red paint.
✦ If you're using the **playlist** recommendations, download the song "Nothing But the Blood" by Matt Redman and ready your iPod or burn a CD in order to play it during the session.

Leader insight:

This study is the first of 9 that will each provide a unique view of the Messiah from a particular part of the Bible—from a person, group, or book of the Bible that serves as a "witness" to who the Messiah is and what he's come to accomplish. But before diving in to these truths about the Messiah, we must start at square one—our deep human need for a solution to our great human problem of sin.

Small group session 1 will help your group face the reality of our sin, explore its effect on all of humanity, and see that the

Bible both profoundly understands the human condition and provides a real, substantive response. This first study focuses on the sacrificial system God set up in the Old Testament and the role of the priest in atoning for the sins of the people. It then explores the true atonement offered by the great High Priest described in Hebrews.

In the Old Testament, the priests facilitated spiritual awareness and health in the Jewish community of faith. The high priest went into the Holy of Holies on the Day of Atonement. In Leviticus 16, we see that Aaron (the high priest) had to tediously follow a code of holiness in order to enter the inner sanctuary so that he could make atonement for himself, his household, and the whole community of Israel. In the New Testament, the author of Hebrews intentionally contrasts the Old Testament high priest with Jesus, saying that Christ "entered the Most Holy Place once for all time and secured our redemption forever" (Hebrews 9:12). Christ's holiness qualifies him for this service. As a result of Christ's sacrifice as the High Priest, we can serve, worship, and have a relationship with "the living God" (9:14). When we understand this new reality that our sins have been fully paid for by Jesus, we should respond by living a drastically changed life.

So what about you? How seriously do you take your own sin—your own part in humanity's biggest problem? Do you understand the gravity of what the High Priest did for you by sacrificing himself? Do you take that truth for granted? As you ready yourself to lead this study, allow some time for yourself to focus on the problem of sin in your own life and the glorious solution the Messiah offers. Invite God to make these truths fresh, new, and life-changing to you.

As you prepare to lead (and join) your kids on this small group adventure, pray: God, thank you for providing a solution to the problem of sin, which plagues all of human-kind and wreaks havoc on my own life. You are the sufficient sacrifice. Jesus, you are the High Priest who atones for me. I am so grateful for your work in my life. Lord, please speak through me as I lead my group in an exploration of sin and your sacrifice. Through these studies, please work in each teen's life—and work in mine as well. In the name of the High Priest, Jesus, I pray. Amen.

b4 u meet

A couple of days before your group meets, send a text message to your kids reminding them of the upcoming Pursue study and get them excited to participate in investigating more about Jesus as the Messiah. (If some teens don't text, send them an e-mail or a message on Facebook or MySpace.)

The Session

Rearrange or delete sections of the study to best meet your group's needs.

txt a frnd `about 2 minutes`

Invite your small group to consider this question:

✸ **What are the best and worst jobs you've ever had to do?**

When they've got an answer, invite them to get out their cell phones and text their answer to another person in the room. (If kids don't have their own phone, they could borrow a friend's or could form pairs and talk about their answer to this question.)

When you're ready to move on to the next part of the study, have them put their cell phones away for now. ✸

mic check `about 7 minutes`

Play this improvisational game, "It's a Party!" based on an activity from the show *Who's Line Is It Anyway?* Get at least 3 volunteer actors. Hand out the assignment and explanation of Party Host to 1 volunteer. Have the other volunteers draw from the remaining descriptions.

Explain that the Party Host will invite people in. The other actors will arrive at the party and interact with one another and the host, saying and doing

It's a Party!

It's a Party!

Party Host: Your job is to figure out the occupations of the guests who are arriving at your party. Watch what they do and listen to what they say to figure them out.

Police officer: You might try to assist someone for something, like booking the party early, not taking enough food, etc. You might say something to the Party Host like, "Do you have a permit to have this many people at your party?"

Firefighter: You might pretend to hose down candles the Party Host lit for ambiance. You might say something like, "Is it hot in here?" (or) smell something burning?"

Carpenter: You might say something like, "This wall doesn't look straight" and lean on to fix it.

Nurse: You might take guests' temperatures or pretend to give them a shot and say, "All better."

Babysitter: You might try to read a book or play a game with some of the guests. You might say something like, "Isn't it your bedtime?"

Fast food restaurant cashier: You might say something like, "Hi, welcome to the party. Your tray is served you?" in a dull, bored voice. You might say, "Do you want fries with that?" when people talk to you.

Teacher: When someone talks to you, you might say, "I was assigned to someone whose hand is raised." You might pretend to teach someone how to do something, such as how to run or do a stand correctly.

Preacher: You might say something like, "God bless you!" and "Amen!" when people talk to you. You might make everyone's hand, put weapons on the back, and pretend to read or quote from the Bible.

pursue • Session 1

Copyright © 2010 Standard Publishing...

things to indicate the job descriptions they've been given. (The job descriptions have some example dialogue and actions for your volunteer actors.) The Party Host will try to figure out what occupation each actor is portraying.

If you only have a few volunteers, you may have them play another round to use more of the descriptions.

Transition by saying: These actors had a tough job today. And they were portraying some tough job professions. Today we'll look at a very difficult job—being a high priest. We'll find out what that is and why Jesus is described as one. ✹

freestyle   about 7-10 minutes

Begin the study by setting the scene for humanity's need for a High Priest:

✹ Most of us are familiar with the beginning of Genesis. God creates the entire earth in 6 days. Genesis 1 goes into detail of what he created each day. Then came the sixth day: "So God created human beings in his own image. In the image of God he created them; male and female he created them" (Genesis 1:27).

✹ Adam and Eve are the only things God created in his own image. And God began a relationship with them. That relationship was like no other part of creation. Obviously, creating people was the culmination of all creation.

At this time, bring out the printout or poster of art you brought. Say something like: Like a priceless work of art, people were his masterpiece. Ask your group:

✹ How does it make you feel to be God's masterpiece?

Then say: But what if someone came along to this piece of art and did this? Now take the black marker and scribble, write words, or draw doodles to ruin the picture. Then say: This is what happened to God's masterpiece—human beings—when they sinned. Your jr. highers are likely familiar with Genesis 3 and the first sin. But if not, give a quick summary. Then ask your group:

✦ How did sin take away from humans' value?
✦ How did sin damage their relationship with their Creator?

Hammer these points home to your kids:

✦ The biggest problem humans face—in all of history and still today—is sin.
✦ Like the artwork, when something of value is defaced, that takes away from its value. Yet we still are able to see the goodness through the junk. So we have hope that it can be restored.

Pass around the scissors and the artwork and ask each kid to cut a piece of the marked-up art. Tell them to see this as themselves—a masterpiece with sin messing up its value. But there's hope that we can be restored.

Explain that over the next 9 studies, your group will be exploring the idea of the Messiah: the solution to humankind's biggest problem. Let them know that *Messiah* means "anointed one," and it is the same word as *Christ* that is used in the New Testament. Let the kids know that every week you'll be looking together at one specific way the Bible describes this Messiah and how he is the only solution for our sin. ✦

solo/strike a chord handout

solo   about 5 minutes

Tell your jr. highers you'd like them to find a spot in your meeting area where they can be alone and spend about 5 minutes reading Scripture and thinking about what it means.

Tell them that you'll first look at the way sin was dealt with in the Old Testament. It wasn't a solution, but it was a step to restoration.

Give each teen a copy of the **solo/strike a chord** handout and a pen or pencil, inviting them to read and follow the instructions. (Have them read through only the top portion, **solo**, right now; they'll need the **strike a chord** portion in a few minutes.) Here's a copy of what they'll read:

Take about 5 minutes to read Leviticus 5:5-10. Consider:
✤ What does all of the blood and death signify about sin?
✤ How does this Scripture passage make you feel?

When the kids understand what they're supposed to do, have them take off and find a spot to read and reflect. After about 5 minutes, call everybody back together. ✤

strike a chord about 10-15 minutes

Discuss what your group read during the **solo** time: Leviticus 5:5-10. Explain that in Old Testament times, the priest's main job was to help the people realize the forgiveness of God through a system of sacrificing animals and other offerings. The priest also played an important role in encouraging people to obey God's laws. Then say: In ancient Israel there was also a high priest. He played a very special role in Israel's sin problem.

Have the group now look at the bottom portion of the **solo/strike a chord** handout and

solo/strike a chord handout

txt it

If you want, invite kids to answer these questions both by talking aloud and by texting. As some share their answers, others can text them to you. Read some of their thoughts aloud and build upon their ideas as your group explores this topic together.

use it to guide your small group Bible exploration and discussion together as a group. Here's a copy of the **strike a chord** text for you to use to guide your discussion time:

Read Leviticus 16:5, 15-17, 20-22 together and talk about these questions:

✦ How would you summarize the high priest's job description in your own words? What does he do? What is he trying to achieve?

✦ How is the high priest representing Israel before God? How is he used by God to address the people's biggest spiritual problem, which we discussed earlier—sin?

Push your group to dig deep. For example get them to discuss, "Why did the priest have to sacrifice the animal?" or "Why was atonement necessary in this way?"

By the end of this time, make sure that your kids understand that the animal sacrifices were made in response to sin. The severity of the animal sacrifices was a response to the seriousness of sin. ✦

encore   about 7-12 minutes

Explain that the book of Hebrews in the New Testament also talks about the high priest. But the interesting thing is that Jesus, the Messiah, is described as the ultimate High Priest.

Go over these key ideas:

✦ From the beginning of time in Genesis 3, we learned that the human problem is sin, and because of this sin we are separated from our Creator. We will never be truly happy until we are brought back into a relationship with our Creator.

* The priest of the Old Testament was never meant to fully address this human spiritual need. The priest merely helped people become more fully aware of the problem.
* Read Hebrews 10:3, which tells us that "those sacrifices actually reminded them of their sins year after year." This means that these animal sacrifices were never meant to fully "take away" the people's sin but instead were to point them toward their need for true spiritual cleansing. As Paul said, "The law simply shows us how sinful we are" (Romans 3:20).
* The Old Testament high priest was a prototype—a sort of symbol—of the coming ultimate solution to the problem of sin.
* It's a different kind of High Priest who will solve humanity's sin problem. This High Priest doesn't sacrifice animals but rather *himself*. Leviticus explained that the animals sacrificed had to be perfect. And the Messiah, our High Priest, was perfect.

txt it

If you want, invite kids to answer these questions both by talking aloud and by texting. As some share their answers, others can text them to you. Read some of their thoughts aloud and build upon their ideas as your group explores this topic together.

Read Hebrews 9:11-15 for your group to show where Jesus is explained as High Priest. Ask:

* Based on this passage, how is the Messiah similar to Old Testament priests? How is he different?
* All this talk about sacrifices and blood can seem strange to our modern way of life. But we must face it—the Messiah died a bloody, brutal death for us. As the High Priest, he was the sacrifice for our sin. What does this make you think or feel?

playlist

To add contemplative ambiance to this prayer experience, download this song to your iPod (or burn to a CD) and play it while kids paint. Encourage them to listen to the words as well.
"Nothing But the Blood" by Matt Redman

backstage pass `about 5-7 minutes`

Bring out your paint, brushes, and roll paper or poster board. Invite your group to come up to the paper and paint the word "Jesus" on the canvas with red paint. As they do, invite them to think about the sacrifice the Messiah made for *them*—for their own sin.

The words can overlap and intersect, smearing into each other. When everyone has participated, it should look like an abstract collage of layered words.

When everybody understands, challenge the group to have a worshipful attitude during this experience, not talking to each other but focusing their thoughts on a private conversation with God. ✦

hit the road `about 2 minutes`

Challenge your jr. highers to let this study really sink in by taking time on their own to seriously consider their own sin—their own part in the big human problem. Encourage them to focus on their own personal need for forgiveness and their own dependence upon the High Priest as the only one who can offer them real forgiveness.

Then conclude the meeting by praying aloud for your kids, using the words of Hebrews 13:20, 21 as your prayer:

"Now may the God of peace—who brought up from the dead our Lord Jesus, the great Shepherd of the sheep, and ratified an eternal covenant with his blood—may he equip you with all you need for doing his will. May he produce in you, through the power of Jesus Christ, every good thing that is pleasing to him. All glory to him forever and ever! Amen."

Let your kids know you'll be sending them **5 for 5 world tour** life application and devotional challenges for them to do each day via Twitter, e-mail, or through a Facebook group you've set up. (Or, if you prefer not to use these technology options, pass out copies of the **5 for 5 world tour** handout you've downloaded from the CD-ROM to the teens.) Encourage your kids to strive to spend about 5 minutes each day connecting with God through these devotional experiences.

aftr u meet

Right after your meeting, send kids the first **5 for 5 world tour** challenge for them to do tomorrow via Twitter, e-mail, or by posting it on a Facebook page (or youth group Web page) you've set up. Continue to send 1 challenge each day for the 5 days following your meeting.

Prompt them to keep at it with their **5 for 5 world tour** challenges and let them know you're praying for them.

5 for 5 world tour

The Messiah as King

— The Prep —

Session goal: Jr. highers will explore the Old Testament expectations of the coming Messiah as a king in the line of David who would usher in a perfect kingdom of righteousness, peace, and justice.

Scriptures: 2 Samuel 7:8-17; Psalm 2; Psalm 89:1-18; Isaiah 9:6, 7

You'll need:

- Bibles
- Pens or pencils
- Spoons (1 per teen)
- 1 bowl
- Cotton balls
- Several hardcover large books
- 2 pieces of poster board
- Colored markers, pens, and highlighters

Download and print:

- "Mark 'Em Up" handout (1 per teen)
- **solo/strike a chord** discussion guide (1 per teen)

Optional supplies:

- For **freestyle** & **backstage pass:** iPod or CD player and CD with recommended **playlist** music.

✦ For **hit the road:** Download and print copies of this week's **5 for 5 world tour** take-home page (1 per teen) if you are unable to use the technology options.

✦ For **freestyle**: You'll need either printouts of Psalm 2 and Psalm 89:1-18 on large sheets of paper (11 x 17 or bigger) to glue to your posters OR you may choose to handwrite the psalms on the posters.

Setting it up:

✦ For **mic check**: Get your room ready for the Royalty Triathlon. Have the books and spoons ready. Fill the bowl half full with cotton balls.

✦ For **freestyle**: Either take the printouts of the 2 psalms listed in the supplies section and glue them onto your 2 pieces of poster board, or handwrite the 2 psalms neatly and largely on the poster board. Place or hang the 2 somewhere in your room where all your kids can easily access them.

✦ If you're using the **playlist** recommendations, download the songs "King" by Tree63, "Here Is Our King" by David Crowder Band, and "King" by Audio Adrenaline. Ready your iPod or burn a CD in order to play the songs during the session.

Leader insight:

One of the richest and most rewarding themes of the Old Testament is the people's expectation of a messianic king who would someday rule on David's throne. Several songs you'll study in this session point to a King who would accomplish what no human king ever could.

The prophets of the Old Testament also spoke often of a coming day of peace and justice that hearkens back to the "good ol' days" of

David's reign. Through Amos, God said, "I will restore the fallen house of David" (Amos 9:11) and, "They will plant vineyards and gardens; they will eat their crops and drink their wine" (9:14), which implied peace. In Ezekiel, God promised, "I will set over them one shepherd, my servant David. He will feed them and be a shepherd to them" (Ezekiel 34:23). This is some 400 years *after* David's time! The obvious point here is that a successor of David would one day bring glory back to God's people. Many of the examples from the Psalms and the prophets cast such an amazing vision that they're clearly capturing a messianic hope. Only the Messiah—no regular human king—could truly fulfill these promises.

A component of the idea of a messianic King is the word *Zion*. It is a poetical and metaphorical moniker for Jerusalem that connotes a whole cluster of positive ideas. It's first used in 2 Samuel 5:7 when David has retaken Jerusalem for his people. Zion represents God's kingdom, which is victorious, righteous, and permanently fixed. Though, geographically speaking, Jerusalem is a modest hill in comparison to the great mountains of the land, theologically speaking it is the most dominant feature on the landscape. Zion is the center of the world, the capital of the earth. Isaiah tells us that "people from all over the world will stream there to worship" (Isaiah 2:2). This means that not only the Jewish people, but all the people of the earth will find their hope in the God of Israel and will be ruled by the messianic King.

When we look at the Old Testament's strong emphasis on a Messiah who would be a conquering king, it's not hard to see why Jesus was rejected by many of the religious teachers and zealots of his time. Rather than a warrior, he was meek and kind. Rather than a "ruler," he lived as a servant. It's as if the meek Jesus came too early for them; they were expecting the Jesus of Revelation. Jesus as servant, described in Isaiah (more in study 3), seemed so different from the Old Testament idea of a Davidic Messiah that they didn't recognize him. Perhaps this is why Jesus so often said, "Anyone with ears to hear should listen and understand" (Matthew 13:9). In other words, the people needed to open their minds to see a humble servant as the Messiah. During his time on earth, Jesus did fulfill some of the kingly promises and prophesies, but Scripture tells us that he will accomplish these things in full in the end, when every knee will bow before him (Philippians 2:10) and his kingdom will be realized (more on this in study 9).

So what about you? What does it mean to you that Jesus is—and will be—the King who makes wrong things right? who finally defeats injustice and evil and sin? who finally brings truth, fairness, goodness, and peace to his people? Do you long for his kingdom as God's people of old longed for the promised messianic King?

In preparation for leading this small group session, spend some time worshiping Jesus as King. Pray: Jesus, you are the King of kings. You've been promised to us from times of old. You're the ruler my heart desires. Let your kingdom come and your will be done on earth and in my life today. And help my jr. highers grasp a vision of the messianic hope your people had in the Old Testament. Help them see how they too should long for you as the true King who will one day rule over all the earth. In Jesus' name, I pray. Amen.

The Session

Rearrange or delete sections of the study to best meet your group's needs.

b4 u meet

A couple of days before your group meets, send a text message to your kids reminding them of the upcoming Pursue study. (If some teens don't text, send them an e-mail or a message on Facebook or MySpace.)

txt a frnd   about 2 minutes

Invite your small group to consider this question:

✦ If you could be king or queen of the world for a day, what's one thing you'd do?

When they've got an answer, invite them to get out their cell phones and text their answer to another person in the room. (If kids don't have their own phone, they could borrow a friend's or could form pairs and talk about their answer to this question.)

When you're ready to move on to the next part of the study, have them put their cell phones away for now. ✦

mic check   about 5-10 minutes

Tell your group you are going to have a Royalty Triathlon. Ask for at least 2 volunteers to participate while others cheer (but the whole group can race if they want). Then introduce the races:

#1—Nobility Ability to Balance: Royalty needs good posture. Give each contestant a book to balance on his or her head. Have the kids perform different tasks—standing on 1 leg, taking 5 steps, turning in a full circle. See who can keep the book balanced the longest.

#2—Stately Silver Spoons: Royalty is often said to be born with a silver spoon in their mouths. Take it literally! Each contestant must hold the end of a spoon in their mouths and must use the spoon

Mark 'Em Up

(no hands!) to scoop all the cotton balls you've placed in a bowl. Fastest person wins.

#3—Majestic Movement: All royalty is required to attend a ball. See how quickly your kids think on their feet. Give each 30 seconds to do an impromptu silly (or talented!) dance. You be the judge on who is the winner!

Congratulate everyone for participating. Then say: Today we're going to look at heavenly royalty as we discover that the Messiah is King. ✹

freestyle `about 10-15 minutes`

Begin by sharing these points with your group:

✦ When we think of our hope as Christians, the symbol we often think of is a cross. But for the ancient Jewish people of the Old Testament, the image was a *throne*. Their hope for salvation from God would be brought about through their king.

✦ The history of the Jewish people is very dark; they were plagued with famine, war, and exile. In their minds, they awaited a powerful, kingly Messiah who would rule and make things right.

Explain that they are now going to look at some messianic psalms in a unique way—by looking closely at the text and marking it up with notes and symbols. Distribute the "Mark 'Em Up" handout to everyone while you explain that you have created 2 posters with 2 different psalms (Psalm 2 and Psalm 89:1-18). Everyone should read both psalms and place marks on them, as explained on the handout.

Encourage your teens to try to make at least 5 different marks or notes on each psalm.

Pass out some markers and highlighters, then send the group out to explore the psalms. Feel free to participate as well. Encourage kids to talk during this activity *if* they're talking about the psalms—but challenge them to stay focused on the project and not talk about other stuff at this time.

After everyone has had a chance to mark each psalm, gather everyone back together and move to **encore** for some discussion questions.

encore [about 5-8 minutes]

Discuss the psalms you marked up during **freestyle**. Ask:

* What stood out to you in these psalms?
* What similarities did you find between the psalms?
* Did you find any important differences?
* Was anything surprising?
* Did you enjoy them? If so, what did you like about them?
* What kind of marks or notes did you make? Why?

You may also want to look on the posters and read a few marks or notes or ask who made certain ones and why. Share your thoughts as well. You might also want to mention:

playlist (part 1)

You may want to play some upbeat rock-style worship songs in the background that celebrate Jesus as King. (The 3 listed are each about 4 minutes. If you don't get through them all now, you can save 1 song for **backstage pass**.) Download these songs to your iPod (or burn to a CD) and play them while kids write on the psalms:
"King" by Tree63
"Here Is Our King" by David Crowder Band
"King" by Audio Adrenaline

txt it

You may want to give your teens the option of texting their answers to these questions to you during your discussion time. Read some of their answers out loud and use them as springboards for further discussion.

hidden track

If you did not just complete **freestyle**, you will need to read these psalms before you begin the discussion: Psalm 2 and Psalm 89:1-18.

solo/strike a chord handout

* These songs express a longing for military victory.
* There is a desire for the nations to recognize the Jewish king as the King of kings.
* All the nations will be subdued by the reign of this mighty King.
* There is an obvious and special relationship between God and this King.
* The King's reign is described as eternal, and it will be characterized by righteousness and justice. *

solo   about 5 minutes

Tell your jr. highers you'd like them to find a spot in your meeting area where they can be alone and spend about 5 minutes reading Scripture and thinking about what it means.

Give each teen a copy of the **solo/strike a chord** handout and a pen or pencil, inviting them to read and follow the instructions. (Have them read through only the top portion, **solo**, right now; they'll need the **strike a chord** portion in a few minutes.) Here's a copy of what they'll read:

Take 5 minutes to read 2 Samuel 7:8-17. Consider:

* What do you think this passage means?
* What stands out to you most from this passage? Why?

When the kids understand what they're supposed to do, have them take off and find a spot to read and reflect. After about 5 minutes, call everybody back together. *

strike a chord `about 10 minutes`

Begin by saying something like this: The focus on a conquering king and a perfect kingdom came because of a specific person—David. Let's look at God's promise to him.

Give the group some context about what has happened so far:

✴ David is on the throne as the second king of Israel.

✴ David has re-conquered Jerusalem from an enemy army, and it is now part of Israel again. Jerusalem is also called Zion and, at this point, the City of David (2 Samuel 5:7). It is an important city for God's people.

✴ David has returned the Ark of God to Jerusalem. It is a sacred symbol of God's presence.

✴ Next we will read about God using the prophet Nathan to make an amazing covenant with David.

txt it

If you want, invite kids to answer these questions both by talking aloud and by texting. As some share their answers, others can text them to you. Read some of their thoughts aloud and build upon their ideas as your group explores this topic together.

Have the group now look at the bottom portion of the **solo/strike a chord** handout and use it to guide your small group Bible exploration and discussion together as a group. Here's a copy of the **strike a chord** text for you to use to guide your discussion time:

Read 2 Samuel 7:8-17 together and talk about these questions:

✴ What stands out to you about God's promises to David?

✴ What's unusual?

✴ Why do you think God blessed David in this way?

✱ What similarities do you see between these verses and the psalms we discussed earlier?

Now look at a portion of David's grateful response to God. Read 2 Samuel 7:25-29.

✱ David believed God's promise, even though he would never live to see the ultimate fulfillment on the throne—Jesus. ✱

backstage pass　about 5 minutes

Say: We find another prophecy about the Messiah as King from Isaiah 9:6, 7.

Instruct your kids to find a partner or 2 and read this Scripture passage together. Then partners should discuss this question: How does the promise of a King personally encourage you in your life and in your faith?

Have kids close this time by praying for one another. ✱

hit the road　about 2 minutes

Wrap up your session today by saying something like this: David was a wonderful king adored by many, but he also sinned and fell short of God's plans for him. His reign didn't last forever, and he wasn't able to bring true and lasting peace to his people. None of the kings who followed did these things either. But we know that the Messiah, Jesus, will return someday and reign as King. We can put our hope in him as the true King of kings.

Close in prayer for your group.

Let your kids know you'll be sending them **5 for 5 world tour** life application and devotional challenges for them to do each day via Twitter, e-mail, or through a Facebook group you've set up. (Or, if you prefer not to use these technology options, pass out copies of the **5 for 5 world tour** handout you've downloaded from the CD-ROM to the teens.) Encourage your kids to strive to spend about 5 minutes each day connecting with God through these devotional experiences. ✦

aftr u meet

Right after your meeting, send kids the first **5 for 5 world tour** challenge for them to do tomorrow via Twitter, e-mail, or by posting it on a Facebook page (or youth group Web page) you've set up. Continue to send 1 challenge each day for the 5 days following your meeting.

Prompt them to keep at it with their **5 for 5 world tour** challenges and let them know you're praying for them.

5 for 5 world tour

The Messiah as Servant

— The Prep —

Session goal: Jr. highers will focus on the Messiah as a Servant who willingly suffered for our sins.

Scriptures: Isaiah 1:2-18; Isaiah 42:1-9; Isaiah 49:1-7; Isaiah 50:4-9; Isaiah 53

You'll need:

- Bibles
- Pens or pencils
- Prepared piece of paper (see **mic check**)
- 1 piece of poster board
- Colored markers

Download and print:

- "Isaiah's Courtroom" handout (3 copies)
- "Servant Songs" handout (1 copy, cut apart)
- **solo/strike a chord** discussion guide (1 per teen)

Optional supplies:

✦ For **encore** & **backstage pass**: iPod or CD player and CD with rec- ommended **playlist** music.
✦ For **hit the road**: Download and print copies of this week's **5 for 5 world tour** take-home page (1 per teen) if you are unable to use the technology options.

Setting it up:

✦ For **mic check**: Write the following rules on a piece of paper so kids will know who wins for this version of Rock-Paper-Scissors:
  • Lawyer beats Jury
  • Jury beats Judge
  • Judge beats Lawyer
✦ For **freestyle**: Draw on your poster board a simple stick figure in black in the middle of the square with the word "Servant" written below it.
✦ For **strike a chord**: Consider where you will have your kids sit to imitate a courtroom. You may want to ask for 3 volunteers before the session begins who can read the parts on the "Isaiah's Court- room" handout. Give the volunteers each a copy of the handout. Have them sit where a Judge, Prosecutor, and Defense Attorney may sit or stand in court. The rest of the group will be the jury.
✦ If you're using the **playlist** recommendations, download these songs from Handel's *Messiah:* Part 2, Number 24, "Surely He Hath Borne Our Griefs" and Part 2, Number 25, "And With His Stripes We are Healed"; also select songs from the album *Seven Swans* by Sufjan Stevens. Ready your iPod or burn a CD in order to play the songs during the session.

Leader insight: ———

Isaiah 40–66 attracts considerable attention from biblical scholars because its subject matter is compelling and it's very different from chapters 1–39. The first half of the book deals primarily with judgment (with some passages on hope sprinkled in); the second half of the book focuses mostly on hope (with some passages on judgment sprinkled in).

The first half of the book establishes the spiritual failings of God's people. For example, Isaiah 1:16 says, "Get your sins out of my sight"; and in 10:1 the prophet states, "What sorrow awaits the unjust judges and those who issue unfair laws."

Then, as if in response to the harsh, corrective nature of the first half of the book, Isaiah introduces *the Servant* in the second half. The Servant beautifully satisfies the promise made in the very first chapter of the book: "Though your sins are like scarlet, I will make them as white as snow" (Isaiah 1:18). We don't know how this promise of forgiveness will happen until the Servant is introduced.

The identity of the Servant is very important for us to understand. First there is a corporate servant (which is Israel), discussed mostly in Isaiah 41:8, 9; 42:19; 44:1; and 45:4. But then we read about the individual, *messianic Servant* of chapters 42:1-9; 49:1-7; 50:4-11; and 52:13–53:12. These passages are called "servant songs"; some scholars believe that Isaiah 61 is a fifth servant song, even though the word *servant* is not used in it.

Our understanding of who the Messiah is becomes more clear as the author makes direct connections between the ideas of the messianic King and the messianic Servant. In Isaiah 42:1, the Servant is linked to the kingly figure from chapters 9 and 11 as God says "I have put my Spirit upon him. He will bring justice to the nations." This harkens back to 9:7, which identified the messianic King as one who will bring justice, and 11:1, which spoke also of the shoot from the stump of Jesse who would be anointed with the Spirit (11:2) and would bring justice (11:4). We can see from these clues that the King and the Servant are one and the same person.

What all this means is that Isaiah gives us the most *full* and striking picture of the Messiah in the Old Testament. Isaiah makes clear the purpose, struggles, divine relationship, character, and victory of the Messiah. The Messiah will not only rule over the earth as King, but will also suffer greatly for our sins in order to bring redemption to his people.

So what about you? How can these words of Isaiah, spoken over 700 years before Christ's birth, speak to you of his purpose? What does it mean to *you* that your sins are washed white as snow? How can you respond to this Messiah, the Servant who suffered on your behalf?

As you prepare to lead this study, pray: Jesus, thank you for being a Servant who gave up everything for us. Please help me to be faithful despite my own struggles and difficulties. Please let my small group kids discover you in a new way this week and appreciate your immense love and sacrifice for them. In your name I pray. Amen.

⁓The Session⁓

Rearrange or delete sections of the study to best meet your group's needs.

txt a frnd `about 2 minutes`

Invite your small group to consider this question:

✴ What's one of the most disobedient things you did as a child? Did you get caught? Did you feel guilty afterward?

When they've got an answer, invite them to get out their cell phones and text their answer to another person in the room. (If kids don't have their own phone, they could borrow a friend's or could form pairs and talk about their answer to this question.)

When you're ready to move on to the next part of the study, have them put their cell phones away for now. ✦

⁓mic check `about 7 minutes`

Have everybody pair up for a unique version of Rock-Paper-Scissors. Instead of the traditional motions, this time kids will play "Lawyer-Jury-Judge." Explain and demonstrate the following motions:

✴ For Lawyer, accusingly point at your opponent and say "Guilty!"
✴ For Jury, scratch your chin and thoughtfully say "Hmmm . . ."
✴ For Judge, pound your fist onto the palm of your other hand (like a gavel) and shout "Order in the court!"

Then explain which motion beats which (and show them the explanation sign you prepared):

b4 u meet

A couple of days before your group meets, send a text message to your kids reminding them of the upcoming Pursue study. (If some teens don't text, send them an e-mail or a message on Facebook or MySpace.)

- Lawyer beats Jury (as in real life: A lawyer persuades the jury to his or her point of view).
- Jury beats Judge (as in real life: A jury ultimately gives the guilty or not guilty sentence, not the Judge).
- Judge beats Lawyer (as in real life: A Judge sets the rules and can even hold a lawyer in contempt of court).

Kids should stand back to back with their opponents, then count to 3. When they say "3!" they should turn and face their opponents, showing their hand motion as either Lawyer, Jury, or Judge.

Once everybody understands, lead the group in playing tournament-style. Have them do a best 2 out of 3 round with their partners. Whoever loses that should sit down, and players should find new partners. Continue leading play in this way until it's down to just one final pair. Whoever wins the final pairing is the winner! If you want, give the winner some candy as a prize.

Say: Let's consider a part of Scripture, viewed as Lawyers and a Judge, and YOU will be the Jury! ✦

Isaiah's Courtroom

strike a chord   about 12 minutes

Ask the kids to get their Bibles and open them to Isaiah 1 while you assign different kids to sit in particular areas to be a courtroom. As you do, tell everybody who's who. Be sure to select good readers to be the Judge, the Prosecutor, and the Defense Attorney, and give each a copy of the "Isaiah's Courtroom" script.

Explain to the group that throughout Isaiah, the prophet uses lots of legal terms and often places the reader in a courtroom-like scene in order to get his point across about human guilt and judgment. For example, read Isaiah 41:1 aloud, which says, "Come now and speak. The court is ready for your case." Introduce your activity:

Let's read parts of Isaiah 1:2-18 to set the scene for this book and our study. But instead of just reading it, let's think of it as a courtroom scene. The Prosecutor, which is the lawyer who is bringing the charge against Israel, will read the lines that accuse God's people of sin. The Judge will respond and give background for the case. The Defense Attorney, which is the lawyer representing Israel, will try to defend God's people.

Have the Prosecutor, Judge, and Defense Attorney read the "Isaiah's Courtroom" script aloud (and do their best to act like a judge and attorneys) while everyone else follows along in their own Bibles.

solo/strike a chord handout

Now give each teen a copy of the **solo/ strike a chord** handout and a pen or pencil. Use the bottom half of the page to guide your small group Bible exploration and discussion together as a group. Here's a copy of the **strike a chord** text for you to use to guide your discussion time:

You just read a lot of Isaiah 1:2-18 together, hearing from the Judge and Lawyers. Discuss these questions as the Jury:

✤ Based on the beginning of Isaiah, what do you expect the entire book to be about?
✤ What seems to be the relationship between Israel, God's people, and God at this point?

* What did the Prosecutor say God accused Israel of doing? (verses 2, 3, 11, 12, 15-17)
* What hope did the Defense Attorney offer from God? (verse 18)
* As the Jury, would you have been as gracious as God and offered Israel a chance to be free? Why or why not?

Explain to your group that Isaiah 1:18 seems strange: After Israel had rejected God, he still said that he would take their sins away. Help your jr. highers consider this paradox with this short activity:

Have the entire group hold out one of their arms straight in front of their faces and make a "thumbs up" sign. Ask them to close one eye, then look out in front of them and place their thumb "over" an object in the room, covering it up in their vision.

Then ask them to switch eyes (without moving their heads or thumbs). Ask: What happened to the object? The objects or their thumbs will have seemed to have moved.

Now, have them open both eyes and keep looking at their thumbs. Ask: What happened now? Their thumbs will look double! This is an object lesson for illustrating the idea of *paradox*.

When we looked from each eye separately, we saw 2 different angles on an object. But putting them together, we are able to see depth. In the same way, last week we looked at Jesus as King, but this week we are going to see him as Servant. How can he be both? Paradox! Both seem contradictory, yet both are true. And they give us depth, like looking through both eyes—we see a deeper view of the Messiah. *

encore

about 20 minutes

Tell the group that Isaiah has 4 passages that are sometimes called "servant songs"—each of these describes the Messiah as a servant and what he will do for God's people. Have your jr. highers break into 2s or 3s and move around the room, discussing the 4 different Scriptures (Isaiah 42:1-9; Isaiah 49:1-7; Isaiah 50:4-9; Isaiah 53) and discussion questions you have placed in various locations.

Have everybody get started at one of the locations. About every 4 minutes, call out "Switch!" then allow about 1 minute for kids to travel to the next corner and get settled before beginning your count of 4 minutes again. When all 4 groups have had discussion time at all 4 areas, invite everybody to gather back together.

freestyle

about 5-8 minutes

Bring out the poster where you have drawn the simple stick figure to represent the Messiah as a simple servant.

Brainstorm with your group song titles for each of these servant songs. Come up with what they would name the songs if they were using these Scriptures to create modern-day

Servant Songs

playlist (part 1)

You may wish to play some background music so that kids won't be distracted by hearing what others are talking about. A great artist to play as background music is Sufjan Stevens from his album *Seven Swans* or some other music of your choosing.

hidden track

If you did not just complete **encore**, you will need to read the following Scriptures before you begin this activity: Isaiah 42:1-9; Isaiah 49:1-7; Isaiah 50:4-9; Isaiah 53.

solo/strike a chord handout

musical hits. Have them write their favorites on the poster surrounding the stick figure. ✹

solo   about 5 minutes

Tell your jr. highers you'd like them to find a spot in your meeting area where they can be alone and spend about 5 minutes reading Scripture and thinking about what it means.

Have your teens now work through the top half of the **solo/strike a chord** handout. Here's a copy of what they'll read:

Take 5 minutes to read Isaiah 53:4, 5. Consider:

✹ What stands out to you most from this passage? Why?

✹ How do you feel knowing that Jesus became a servant to the point of dying for our sins?

When the kids understand what they're supposed to do, have them take off and find a spot to read and reflect. ✹

backstage pass   about 5 minutes

If you just completed **solo**, ask your kids to stay in their spread out spots. If you didn't, have your group spread out on their own at this time.

Tell your group that they are going to listen to 2 songs about Jesus from Handel's *Messiah*. Let them know that although this music was written over 250 years ago, it still speaks to us today. Ask them to focus on the words and the message these songs share of the Messiah being a Servant who makes the ultimate sacrifice.

Ask your kids to turn over to the back of their **solo** papers and write out the words of Isaiah 53:4, 5 onto their papers as the music plays (in doing so, ingraining the powerful meaning of the words into their minds) and then perhaps writing a sentence in their own words, such as: "He did it for me. He was killed because of my sin."

Now play the 2 songs listed in the margin in the **playlist**. These take about 5 minutes total. ✦

playlist (part 2)

For this activity, you will need to download and play the following songs:
Handel's *Messiah,* Part 2, Number 24, "Surely He Hath Borne Our Griefs"
Handel's *Messiah,* Part 2, Number 25, "And With His Stripes We are Healed"

hit the road   about 1 minute

Read one more verse in Isaiah about the Servant Messiah. Isaiah 61:1: "The Spirit of the Sovereign LORD is upon me, for the LORD has anointed me to bring good news to the poor. He has sent me to comfort the brokenhearted and to proclaim that captives will be released and prisoners will be freed."

Say: Isaiah prophesied that the Messiah would go through terrible suffering for you and me. Why would he do it? To bring us good news. To bind up and heal our hearts. To set us free from sin.

Challenge your kids to spend time this week thinking about the personal difference it makes in their life to know that the Messiah suffered for them. Encourage them to find joy and peace in the complete forgiveness the Messiah offers.

Let your kids know you'll be sending them **5 for 5 world tour** life application and devotional challenges for them to do each day via Twitter, e-mail, or through a Facebook group you've set up. (Or, if you prefer not to use these technology options, pass out copies of the **5 for 5 world tour** handout you've downloaded from the CD-ROM to the

aftr u meet

Right after your meeting, send kids the first **5 for 5 world tour** challenge for them to do tomorrow via Twitter, e-mail, or by posting it on a Facebook page (or youth group Web page) you've set up. Continue to send 1 challenge each day for the 5 days following your meeting.

Prompt them to keep at it with their **5 for 5 world tour** challenges and let them know you're praying for them.

5 for 5 world tour

teens.) Encourage your kids to strive to spend about 5 minutes each day connecting with God through these devotional experiences.

The Messiah as Son of God

The Prep

Session goal: Jr. highers will discover what it means that the Messiah was both fully human and fully divine.

Scriptures: Mark 1:1, 9-11; Mark 3:10, 11; Mark 5:1-7; Mark 9:2-8; Mark 14:32-36, 55-64; Mark 15:37-39; Philippians 2:5-11; Hebrews 2:14, 15

You'll need:

- Bibles
- Pens or pencils
- A few rolls of tape
- Paper—white or colored (1 or 2 sheets per teen)
- Art supplies: colored pencils, markers, or crayons (some for each teen)

Download and print:

- **solo/strike a chord** discussion guide (1 per teen)

Optional supplies:

* For **mic check** (option 1): Download and print the "A Little Bit About Me" handout. Print 1 or 2 copies, enough so that each teen in your group can have 3 "I am . . ." squares.
* For **mic check** (option 2): magazine ads or other printouts with pictures of people kids won't recognize.
* For **backstage pass**: iPod or CD player and CD with recommended **playlist** music.
* For **hit the road**: Download and print copies of this week's **5 for 5 world tour** take-home page (1 per teen) if you are unable to use the technology options.

Setting it up:

* For **mic check** (option 1): Cut apart the "I am . . ." squares from the "A Little Bit About Me" handout and have them available. Also have several rolls of tape handy for the game.
* For **mic check** (option 2): Select 3 or 4 pictures from magazines or print photos you find online that prominently feature one person— but *not* someone famous or recognizable. Get these ready to show to your group.
* Set out the art supplies you brought so that every kid can take some to use during **backstage pass**.
* If you're using the **playlist** recommendations, download the songs "Son of God" by Starfield and "Son of God" by Lincoln Brewster and ready your iPod or burn a CD in order to play the songs during the session.

Leader insight:

"This is the Good News about Jesus the Messiah, the Son of God" (Mark 1:1). To those of us in the church, these words feel familiar and safe. Of course Jesus is the Son of God! It's a phrase we're used to hearing.

But when Mark wrote these words, they were audacious, bold, and world-shaking. Mark starts out his Gospel with this point and bookends it with the same declaration from the centurion: "This man truly was the Son of God!" (Mark 15:39). To claim that Jesus was the very Son of God was not a small thing!

In this study, you'll introduce kids to one of the most essential ideas of Christianity: The Messiah, Jesus, was both fully God and fully human. To truly know Jesus, we must hold both of these ideas in balance.

People have had imbalanced views of Jesus from very early on in the history of Christianity. By the second century AD, a view called *docetism* had begun to spread. Docetism viewed Jesus as not truly human; instead it asserted that he just *appeared* to be human. On the flip side was an idea called *arianism,* which grew in popularity in the fourth century AD. Arianism denied that Jesus was fully God, asserting that as God's Son he was somehow less than God himself.

Though people may not commonly use the terms *docetism* and *arianism* today, these heretical ideas still persist. Many people still have a view of Jesus that diminishes his divinity (or disbelieves it entirely). Lots of people say they like Jesus and are attracted to his teachings, but they view him as merely a good teacher or a prophet or someone who was extremely "spiritual." They don't recognize him as God, thus leaving him with very little authority to speak into their lives.

Without realizing it, even well-meaning Christians can develop a view of Jesus as not quite human. They focus so much on his divinity and authority that it's as if he's some floating, mystical being always wearing a halo and surrounded by a glowing light. When this error is made, people lose sight of the amazing truth of the Incarnation: Jesus became one of us, he knows how we feel, and he can relate intimately to us.

It's essential that we understand and believe the truth about Jesus as he really is, however paradoxical and mysterious it seems. As God he is our authority and we are compelled to obey him. He's all-powerful, thus we can trust him fully. He's all-knowing, thus we can turn to him with our questions. And as a man, Jesus knows what our life is like. He's faced temptation and he's suffered. He's experienced the full range of human emotion. Because he's been one of us, we can turn to him not as a distant God far off in the universe, but as an intimate friend. We can truly connect with him because he can relate to us.

So what about you? Are you too familiar with Jesus' title as the Son of God? Do you take these truths about his nature—his full divinity and full humanity—for granted? How can you meet Jesus afresh through Mark's eyes? How can you relate more closely to Jesus as a human being? How can you turn to Jesus more sincerely when you face challenges, trusting in his power and authority as the God of the universe?

In preparation for leading this small group study, pray: Jesus, you are the Son of God. You were a human like me. And you are God himself. Help me to relate to you more intimately and to trust you more fully. And open the eyes of my kids as they come to discover these same truths about you. In your name, Amen.

b4 u meet

A couple of days before your group meets, send a text message to your kids reminding them of the upcoming Pursue study. (If some teens don't text, send them an e-mail or a message on Facebook or MySpace.)

The Session

Rearrange or delete sections of the study to best meet your group's needs.

txt a frnd
about 2 minutes

Invite your small group to consider this question:

❋ Did you have a nickname as a child? Did you like it? Why or why not? If you didn't, what's a nickname that would fit you better?

When they've got an answer, invite them to get out their cell phones and text their answer to another person in the room. (If kids don't have their own phone, they could borrow a friend's or could form pairs and talk about their answer to this question.)

When you're ready to move on to the next part of the study, have them put their cell phones away for now. ❋

mic check (option 1)
about 7-10 minutes

A Little Bit About Me

I am . . .	I am . . .	I am . . .
I am . . .	I am . . .	I am . . .
I am . . .	I am . . .	I am . . .
I am . . .	I am . . .	I am . . .
I am . . .	I am . . .	I am . . .
I am . . .	I am . . .	I am . . .
I am . . .	I am . . .	I am . . .
I am . . .	I am . . .	I am . . .

A Little Bit About Me

pursue · Session 4

Pass out a pen and 3 "I am . . ." squares to each kid from the "A Little Bit About Me" handout and ask them to come up with 3 truthful statements about themselves. Ask them to avoid general statements such as "I am a guy" or "I am 13." Instead, they should write short, specific descriptions of themselves such as "I am into soccer," "I am a red-head," "I am addicted to my Wii," "I am Italian-American," "I am adopted," or "I am in Mr. Jones' pre-Algebra class." Kids should *not* write their names on their squares and should *not* show anyone.

When everybody's done writing, collect the squares and shuffle them well. Next, pass out the squares again, giving 3 to each kid. Also have available several rolls of tape.

hidden track

There are 2 **mic check** options for you. Pick the activity that best fits your group.

Explain Round 1 of the game: The kids should read their new squares and try to guess who each belongs to. They should go and tape the squares on the backs of people who may have written the statements. The catch? No one can talk or ask questions. Also, each player can only end up with 3 squares taped on his or her back. If someone's back already has 3 squares taped on, no additional squares can be added. At the end of this round, all players should have 3 squares on their backs.

When everybody understands these rules, start Round 1. After a few minutes, have everyone finish. Then get your kids to check the squares on their backs. If a square is correct, they should tape it back on. If a square is incorrect, they should hold onto it for Round 2.

When everybody's ready, lead a quick Round 2 of this game: This time, kids *can* talk to each other, ask and answer questions (truthfully!), and give each other suggestions. The game ends when all players have their original 3 squares taped to their backs.

After the game, ask your group:

✴ Did you think this game was easy or hard? Why?

✴ How well did the squares people taped onto you fit with who you really are? Explain.

mic check (option 2)   about 5 minutes

Have everybody gather near you and show your group several pictures of various people they don't know and won't recognize. Let the group see each picture for just 2 to 3 seconds.

After you've shown them the pictures, invite the group to imagine that they're witnesses of a crime involving those people. How well could they describe each person to the police? Lead the group in brainstorming important details they observed and sharing descriptions of each person.

When they've done their best describing each person, show them the pictures again and have them judge how well they were able to describe each person. Point out any important details about each person that they may have missed or overlooked. Ask the group:

✸ If you were really a witness and had to describe these people, how well would you rate your job of describing them?

✸ Now imagine instead that you had to describe your brother or sister or mom or dad. How well do you think you'd do describing them?

Point out that they could probably describe their family members extremely well because they see them daily and know them intimately. ✸

encore   about 2-3 minutes

Transition from the opening activity by pointing out that, just like there are people we know very well and people who know us well, there were people who lived with Jesus, who saw him day in and day out, and who really knew him. These people were eyewitnesses to who he was, what he was like, what he said, and what he did. Just as we can know and describe our closest friends and family members, these key witnesses could describe Jesus very, very well.

Introduce your study time with some thoughts about the 4 Gospels that you are going to look through during the next few small group sessions:

- ✦ The first 4 books of the New Testament are called the Gospels and are first-century witnesses of the Messiah: Jesus.
- ✦ The Gospel writers wrote about their own experiences with Jesus as well as the accounts shared with them by others. But these weren't just memoirs—the writers were guided by God's Holy Spirit as they wrote. They were inspired by God.
- ✦ All of these Gospels contain the stories and teachings of Jesus and were "published" when many people who had witnessed the events recorded in them were still alive. If anything in the Gospels had been incorrect, there would have been plenty of people around who'd witnessed these events and could have pointed out the errors. But this didn't happen. We can take these accounts to be completely accurate because no one who'd seen Jesus in action refuted them.
- ✦ All 4 Gospels have the same goal of portraying the events and teachings of Jesus' life. But each author also emphasized somewhat different things. When taken together, the 4 different voices give us a full picture of just who this Messiah—Jesus—really was.

Let the group know that in this study you'll be looking specifically at the Gospel of Mark and what it has to say about the Messiah. (You'll look at the other 3 Gospels over the next few weeks.) ✦

hidden track

The **encore** section appears earlier than usual to help give your group background on the Gospels that you will be studying the next few sessions.

solo   about 5 minutes

Tell your jr. highers you'd like them to find a spot in your meeting area where they can

be alone and spend about 5 minutes reading Scripture and thinking about what it means.

Tell them that this small group session will focus on the Gospel of Mark, and the author tells us the main goal of his Gospel account right off the bat. They'll read about it now.

Give each teen a copy of the **solo/strike a chord** handout and a pen or pencil, inviting them to read and follow the instructions. (Have them read through only the top portion, **solo**, right now; they'll need the **strike a chord** portion in a few minutes.) Here's a copy of what they'll read:

Take 5 minutes to read Mark 1:1, 9-11 and Mark 9:2-8. Consider:

✴ What does it seem like Mark is emphasizing in this Gospel?

✴ What's so important about what God the Father says about Jesus?

When the kids understand what they're supposed to do, have them take off and find a spot to read and reflect. After about 5 minutes, call everybody back together. ✴

strike a chord `about 15 minutes`

Read Mark 1:1 aloud, then emphasize that Mark is written to declare one key truth about Jesus: He is the Son of God.

Have the group now look at the bottom portion of the **solo/strike a chord** handout and use it to guide your small group Bible exploration and discussion together as a group. Here's a copy of the **strike a chord** text for you to use to guide your discussion time:

There are 4 key witnesses about Jesus in Mark that point out the same important idea: Jesus is the Son of God. You just read about the first witness in your **solo** time. Read the other passages together with your group. Once you've read them all, use the questions below to talk about them.

God as a witness: Mark 1:9-11 and Mark 9:2-8
Demons as witnesses: Mark 3:10, 11 and Mark 5:1-7
Jesus himself as a witness: Mark 14:32-36 and Mark 14:55-64
A Roman guard as a witness: Mark 15:37-39

✤ Today we're used to hearing the phrase "Son of God" to describe Jesus. But step back in time for a moment and imagine you lived in Jesus' time. What would it mean for someone to say that about another human being? What would your reaction be to hear someone claim that about himself?

✤ Why does it matter that the demons said Jesus was the Son of God? What's the importance of that?

✤ Why does it matter that God the Father declared Jesus was his Son?

✤ Why do you think it's important that a guard who was part of Jesus' execution team (not a disciple) said this about Jesus?

txt it

If you want, invite kids to answer these questions both by talking aloud and by texting. As some share their answers, others can text them to you. Read some of their thoughts aloud and build upon their ideas as your group explores this topic together.

hidden track

In Mark 14:36, Jesus calls God *"Abba,"* which is equivalent to our word "Daddy." This shows that he wasn't just referring to God with a formal title of "Father," but was really talking to his "Dad."

backstage pass about 15-20 minutes

Before you begin this reflection activity, go over these points:

✦ Explain to the group that there are 2 main titles for Jesus that are emphasized in Mark: "Son of Man" and "Son of God." Jesus often called himself the "Son of Man," which simply meant that he was human. "Son of God" means that he claimed to be *God*. Both titles for Jesus are true: He was both God and human.

✦ Tell the group that the theological term for this is the *incarnation*. The Bible teaches that Jesus was God incarnate, which literally means God "in flesh."

✦ Use DNA as a metaphor to help kids think about this: Explain that we get our traits—our hair color, our eye color, our height, our skin color, and more—from our biological mom and dad. We get half of our chromosomes from one parent and half from the other. So in essence, we're basically 50-50 of our biological parents.

✦ Emphasize that with Jesus, things were different. He wasn't 50 percent God and 50 percent human. If we thought he was only "half God," it'd be like he only had half the power or half the divinity. And he wasn't "half human" either—he didn't experience only half of what it's like to be a person. Jesus was *both* 100 percent human and 100 percent God. It's illogical. It's mysterious. But it's true.

Now, invite everyone to grab some of the art supplies you set out (paper, drawing and writing utensils), and let your group know that they're going to have some time to sketch, doodle, or write their own thoughts.

Once kids have each gotten some supplies, prompt them to spread out around the room where they can have their own space. When everybody is settled, explain that for the next few moments, you are going to read some things aloud, and you want them to think about what the ideas mean to them personally. Encourage them to connect with God and to think about their own questions, thoughts, and ideas, creatively expressing to God whatever comes to mind.

Invite kids to prayerfully listen as you read the following words of reflection; if they want, they can begin drawing or writing as you talk.

Say: Why does it matter that Jesus was fully human?

Just like us, Jesus was born. He was a child. He learned to walk and talk. He grew. He was a teenager. He went through the ups and downs of teenage life. He eventually became an adult. Just like us, Jesus ate. He probably had favorite foods that he enjoyed. Just like us, Jesus needed sleep. He got tired and worn out. He needed time alone to relax and be refreshed. Just like us, Jesus felt pain. When he skinned his knee as a kid, it bled and stung. When he was nailed to a cross, it hurt unbelievably. Just like us, Jesus laughed. He had friends. He probably sang and danced and celebrated with them. Like us, Jesus experienced all sorts of human emotions—fear, betrayal, joy, hurt, delight, temptation. Jesus was a human . . . just like me . . . just like **you**.

Read Hebrews 2:14, 15 aloud to the group, and ask: Why does it matter to you that Jesus was fully human?

Invite kids to respond by writing (journaling thoughts, jotting down random words, creating a poem) or drawing (sketching images, doodling things, creating something abstract). Allow about 3 to 5 minutes for kids to write or draw at this point.

Next invite everyone to prayerfully listen as you read these words of reflection (continuing to draw or write if they want): Why does it matter that Jesus was fully God?

playlist

To set a worshipful tone for this reflection time, download these songs to your iPod (or burn to a CD) and play them (in this order) while kids create. Encourage them to listen to the words as well.
"Son of God" by Starfield
"Son of God" by Lincoln Brewster

As a human, Jesus understands our needs. As God, he is able to help us. He has power and authority over sin—he can forgive us. He has power and authority over Satan—he can protect us. He has power and authority over all of creation—he holds all of the universe, including every aspect of our lives, in his hand.

Read Philippians 2:5-11 and say: Jesus wasn't just a good guy who taught good things. He wasn't just someone who was "close" to God. He was God himself.

Why does it matter to *you* that Jesus was fully God?

Direct your kids to respond again through a time of writing or drawing for the remaining 3 to 5 minutes. After this time, have them gather together to either discuss the questions in **freestyle** or move to the ending challenge, **hit the road**. 🟥

freestyle　about 5 minutes

If you just finished the writing/drawing activity, invite kids to spend some time sharing their thoughts from that creative reflection experience. If they feel comfortable, kids can share what they wrote or draw; if they prefer to keep their creation private, that's fine.

Whether you did the writing/drawing activity or not, you can discuss these questions:

🟥 What difference does it make in your life that Jesus was totally human?

🟥 What difference does it make for you that Jesus is fully God? 🟥

txt it

You may want to give your teens the option of texting their answers to these questions to you during your discussion time. Read some of their answers out loud and use them as springboards for further discussion.

hit the road　about 1 minute

Take a moment to summarize the key points of the study, especially drawing attention to any important insights kids shared during your discussion times. Reiterate the key idea that the Gospel of Mark emphasizes over and over again: Jesus is the Son of God. This isn't just a truth we believe in our minds—it's a truth that should shape the entire way we relate to Jesus. Because he was human, Jesus knows and understands how we really feel and can always understand what we're going through. As God, we can put our full trust in him. He is powerful, faithful, and true.

Challenge your kids to move beyond just intellectually acknowledging this truth about Jesus and truly begin acting on it by growing in their own intimacy with Jesus. Encourage them to focus specifically on their prayer life by more regularly turning to Jesus with their needs and speaking openly and honestly to him as an intimate friend.

Wrap up the study by leading the group in a closing prayer.

Let your kids know you'll be sending them **5 for 5 world tour** life application and devotional challenges for them to do each day via Twitter, e-mail, or through a Facebook group you've set up. (Or, if you prefer not to use these technology options, pass out copies of the **5 for 5 world tour** handout you've downloaded from the CD-ROM to the teens.) Encourage your kids to strive to spend about 5 minutes each day connecting with God through these devotional experiences. ✹

aftr u meet

Right after your meeting, send kids the first **5 for 5 world tour** challenge for them to do tomorrow via Twitter, e-mail, or by posting it on a Facebook page (or youth group Web page) you've set up. Continue to send 1 challenge each day for the 5 days following your meeting.

Prompt them to keep at it with their **5 for 5 world tour** challenges and let them know you're praying for them.

5 for 5 world tour

The Messiah
as Lord

The Prep

Session goal: Jr. highers will be challenged to truly recognize Jesus as Lord of their lives as they examine the difference between genuine and shallow faith.

Scriptures: Matthew 7:21-27; Matthew 8:1-3, 5-10, 23-27; Matthew 13:1-9, 18-23; Matthew 21:1-3

You'll need:

- ✦ Bibles
- ✦ Pens or pencils
- ✦ 8 to 10 prepared signs (paper or pieces of poster board)
- ✦ Sheets of dot stickers (about 2 sheets per teen, available at office supply stores)
- ✦ Colored sidewalk chalk (about 1 piece for every 2 teens)
- ✦ 2 potted plants
- ✦ A bowl
- ✦ A few spoons
- ✦ String or yarn cut into 6-inch pieces (1 piece per teen)
- ✦ Video game controller

Download and print:

- ✦ "Solid or Shallow?" handout (1 per teen)
- ✦ **solo/strike a chord** discussion guide (1 per teen)

Optional supplies:

- ✤ For **mic check:** a video game system and television.
- ✤ For **backstage pass** & **encore:** iPod or CD player and CD with recommended **playlist** music.
- ✤ For **backstage pass** & **encore:** bricks, cinderblocks, or rocks if you are unable to meet outside.
- ✤ For **hit the road:** Download and print copies of this week's **5 for 5 world tour** take-home page (1 per teen) if you are unable to use the technology options.

Setting it up:

- ✤ For **mic check:** Create 8 to 10 signs and hang them up around your room. Write one of the following phrases on each sign: your school, the country, the President, your family, your state, your friends, your parents, and your favorite sports team, your extra-curricular group, etc. You might create signs with specific names of sports teams or other local things that your kids would be loyal to.
- ✤ For **backstage pass** & **encore:** Set up 2 stations for the "Solid or Shallow" Scripture stations.

Station 1 should ideally be in an outdoor area where kids can write directly on concrete or asphalt with chalk (like a parking lot, driveway, or sidewalk). If weather doesn't permit you to have kids go outside, find an indoor spot where kids can access concrete, such as a concrete floor in an unfinished basement, furnace room, or garage. (If none of these options works for you, bring in some bricks, cinderblocks, or rocks that kids can write on.)

Station 2 can be inside or outside. Set out 1 potted plant, several spoons, all the pieces of string, and a bowl for kids to scoop the dirt into. (Save the second plant for the second group of kids.)

* If you're using the **playlist** recommendations, download the songs "Jesus is Lord" by Bethany Dillon & Mark Hammitt and "Lord Over All" by Sonicflood and ready your iPod or burn a CD in order to play the songs during the session.

Leader insight:

The Gospel of Matthew (attributed to the tax collector of Matthew 9:9) was written primarily to a Jewish-Christian audience, and it strongly emphasizes a markedly Jewish Messiah in a distinctly Jewish context using Jewish language.

So it shouldn't surprise us that Matthew gives a lot of attention to the different Jewish religious sects. In Matthew, the Pharisees are regularly and sharply contrasted with authentic believers. Several times throughout the book we see the harsh criticism of the religious leaders and an emphasis on real faith found in the marginalized, in the outsiders. In Matthew 9:11 the Pharisees say, "Why does your teacher eat with such scum?" Jesus responds by saying, "Healthy people don't need a doctor—sick people do" (9:12). In 12:38, when they ask for a sign from Jesus, he fires back, "Only an evil, adulterous generation would demand a miraculous sign" (12:39). In chapter 21, Jesus subversively attacks the Pharisees in a parable about unfaithful tenants. And, climatically, in chapter 23, on the Tuesday before his crucifixion, Jesus repeatedly calls them hypocrites. He satirizes their religious practices and exposes their empty faith.

In contrast to this example of false faith, Jesus stresses the idea of genuine faith repeatedly in Matthew. He calls mere fisherman to follow him, he gravitates to the outcasts, and favors the centurion's expressed faith in Matthew 8:10, even though he's a Gentile. Jesus was obviously more concerned with internal faith rather than an external, showy façade of belief. The Parables of the Sower and the Builder illustrate the point further. It was *real* faith that Jesus was concerned with. The term *Lord* used throughout Matthew summarizes this real authentic faith—a faith that truly lives under Jesus' lordship.

Jesus is addressed as Lord multiple times throughout the Gospel of Matthew. Among these, the most notable instances are the leper in Matthew 8:2, the centurion in 8:6, the 2 blind men in 9:28, Peter in 14:28, and the Canaanite mother in 15:22. Jesus refers to himself as Lord several times too. Each one of these examples appeals to the authority of Jesus and his divine position. In contrast to the faithless Pharisees, people called Jesus Lord as an expression of sincere faith. According to Matthew, lordship is a natural corollary of salvation. Someone who is following Christ *must* have a clear and proper understanding of Jesus as the supreme God. *Lord* is truly a term of faith.

So what about you? As a youth leader, you're constantly looked to as an example by your kids, so the temptation is always there: the temptation to focus too much on the outward appearance of your faith (like the Pharisees) rather than devoting the energy and focus needed to live a complete faith (both inward *and* outward) that is surrendered entirely to Jesus. Think anew this week about what it means for you to call Jesus "Lord." Whenever you use the word in prayer or conversation, really mean it. Let it sink in afresh that Jesus is the Lord of all you are.

In preparation for leading this small group session, pray: Lord Jesus, you are in command over all your creation . . . and over every aspect of my life. Please help me to become more aware of your position over my life and help the kids in my ministry discover this truth in a fresh way. I pray that we may all respond appropriately to your grace in love, discipline, and righteousness. Amen.

The Session

Rearrange or delete sections of the study to best meet your group's needs.

mic check anytime before the session begins

If you have time before your small group session begins and you have a TV and video game system available, you may want to have your teens play for a few minutes. Have each kid only play one game and then others should take a turn. Encourage the others to cheer on the players and be involved as spectators.

At the end of the session, this video game time will become an object lesson for your group to consider. ✶

txt a frnd about 2 minutes

Invite your small group to consider this question:

✶ Think of all the things you did last week—the people you spent time with, the activities you did at school, the things you did in the evenings, etc. Which of these was the most important to you? Why?

When they've got an answer, invite them to get out their cell phones and text their answer to another person in the room. (If kids don't have their own phone, they could borrow a friend's or could form pairs and talk about their answer to this question.)

When you're ready to move on to the next part of the study, have them put their cell phones away for now. ✶

b4 u meet

A couple of days before your group meets, send a text message to your kids reminding them of the upcoming Pursue study. (If some teens don't text, send them an e-mail or a message on Facebook or MySpace.)

hidden track

You may have a kid who loves to goof off and who will be tempted to put way more than 3 dot stickers on a given sign. Keep an eye on what's going on at the signs and try to prevent that from happening because it will mess up the tally.

txt it

You may want to give your teens the option of texting their answers to these questions to you during your discussion time. Read some of their answers out loud and use them as springboards for further discussion.

freestyle `about 10 minutes`

Pass out a sheet of dot stickers to each kid and point out the signs you've posted on one wall of your meeting room, such as: your school, the country, the President, your family, your state, your friends, your parents, your favorite sports team, your extra-curricular group, etc.

Explain that you'd like kids to go to each sign and put some dot stickers on it to indicate how much loyalty they have toward that given person, group, or thing. They can put 0-3 stickers: 0 if they feel no loyalty at all; 1 or 2 stickers if they feel a small or medium amount of loyalty; and 3 stickers if they have a high amount of loyalty.

When everybody understands, have kids start marking up the signs with their dot stickers.

Have the kids sit down when they're done voting with their dots. When everybody is finished, have them help you tally up the number of dots on each sign and write down the scores. Then ask the group:

* Do the scores surprise you in any way? How?
* Which item did you feel most loyal to? Why?
* Which item did you feel least loyal to? Why?
* What does it mean to be loyal?
* What kinds of things are you willing to do for someone or something you are loyal to? What sacrifices are you willing to make for that person or thing? ✹

solo `about 5 minutes`

Tell your jr. highers you'd like them to find a spot in your meeting area where they can be alone and spend about 5 minutes reading Scripture and thinking about what it means.

Tell them that this small group session will focus on the Gospel of Matthew, specifically looking at Jesus as Lord.

Give each teen a copy of the **solo/strike a chord** handout and a pen or pencil, inviting them to read and follow the instructions.

(Have them read through only the top portion, **solo**, right now; they'll need the **strike a chord** portion in a few minutes.) Here's a copy of what they'll read:

Take 5 minutes to read Matthew 7:21-23. Consider:

❧ How does this passage make you feel?

❧ What kind of person do you think would call Jesus "Lord," yet not actually obey him?

When the kids understand what they're supposed to do, have them take off and find a spot to read and reflect. After about 5 minutes, call everybody back together. ❧

strike a chord `about 10-15 minutes`

Use the concept of medieval knights as an illustration to talk more about the idea of loyalty. Explain the following key ideas:

❧ In Europe during the medieval times or Middle Ages (from about the fifth century through the sixteenth century), there was a political system in place called the feudal system. In this system, there would be a lord who owned a large area of land. Everything in that land, from the homes to the farms and even the people living there, in essence belonged to him.

* Knights were warriors who would swear *fealty* to their lord. *Fealty* means faithfulness. The lord of a certain area would give the knight some property and also some freedom to live as he saw fit. But in his oath of fealty, the knight declared his total and complete loyalty to his lord. He affirmed that his property and livelihood all ultimately belonged to his lord.

* In his oath of fealty, the knight also promised that if called upon, he would go to battle for his lord. He promised that he'd give his very life if he needed to in order to fight for his lord. It was the ultimate pledge of loyalty.

* In English, our word *lord* comes from this medieval system. A lord is someone who owns everything you have—even your life. A lord is someone you'd even die for if called upon.

Have the group now look at the bottom portion of the **solo/strike a chord** handout and use it to guide your small group Bible exploration and discussion together as a group. Here's a copy of the **strike a chord** text for you to use to guide your discussion time:

Read the following passages of Scripture together and note the situations when people called Jesus "Lord." Also note the different people who called him that.

* Matthew 8:1-3
* Matthew 8:5-10
* Matthew 8:23-27
* Matthew 21:1-3

Now discuss the following as a group:

✦ These are just a few examples in Matthew's Gospel of people who called Jesus "Lord." What do you think each person meant as he or she said "Lord"?

✦ What similarities and differences are there between the way "lord" was used in medieval times, or even today, and how it was used when people spoke to Jesus?

✦ How often have you called Jesus "Lord"? Have you ever fully thought about what it meant? ✦

txt it

If you want, invite kids to answer these questions both by talking aloud and by texting. As some share their answers, others can text them to you. Read some of their thoughts aloud and build upon their ideas as your group explores this topic together.

backstage pass & encore   about 20-25 minutes

Say something like this to your group: We're pretty used to using the word *Lord* for Jesus. Many Christians say "Lord" as if it's a nickname for Jesus. We may not even pay attention to what it truly means. Simply calling him "Lord" doesn't mean we get it. Calling him "Lord" isn't enough. We have to have a genuine faith to back it up.

Tell your group they are going to spend some time examining 2 parables that discuss genuine vs. superficial faith. Divide the group into 2 smaller groups. Give each kid a copy of "Solid or Shallow?" and have them take their Bibles to the 2 stations you set up earlier.

Here's a quick overview of what they'll be doing at each station:

✦ At Station 1 kids will read Jesus' parable about a house built upon the sand and a house built on a good foundation in Matthew 7:21-27. They'll explore what this story means

Solid or Shallow?

playlist

If you want to play some songs that focus on Jesus as Lord while kids are working at the stations, download these songs to your iPod (or burn to a CD).
"Jesus is Lord" by Bethany Dillon & Mark Hammitt
"Lord Over All" by Sonicflood

hidden track

You may want to come up with some of your own responses before-hand to these questions so that you can get the discussion started.

txt it

If you want, invite kids to answer these questions both by talking aloud and by texting. As some share their answers, others can text them to you. Read some of their thoughts aloud and build upon their ideas as your group explores this topic together.

and what it reveals about genuine faith. Then they'll use sidewalk chalk to write their answers to one of the questions on cement.

* At Station 2 kids will explore the Parable of the Sower in Matthew 13:1-9, 18-23. They'll discuss what the story means and will zero in on the shallow and unfruitful kinds of faith Jesus refers to. They'll think about what shallow and unfruitful faith is like in jr. high life. Then they'll act out the parable in 2 ways using a potted plant: They'll tie strings tightly around the stem to represent faith-chokers and will dig out some of the soil to represent shallow faith. (There should be 2 potted plants at this station; you should set out 1 plant for each group that comes to the station.)

After kids have had time to work through the items and questions at each station, gather them back together and discuss the questions on the handouts.

Close this section by saying something like this: Jesus doesn't want us to just call him "Lord." What he wants is for us to do God's will.

hit the road   `about 5 minutes`

Remind the group of the video games they played at the start of the lesson. (If they didn't play during this small group time, have them think about the last time they played a video game.) Use the experience as an illustration of lordship.

Hold up a video game controller. Explain the basic idea that in a video game, the character (or object) on the screen does *not* act on its own. It only does what it is told or commanded to do by the player through the controller. In essence, the player is the lord or master over the character in the game.

Ask: How is Jesus being our Lord like a video game? How is it different? Point out that God gives us free will, so he doesn't force us to do things like the video game controller. He lets us choose to serve him as Lord.

Then have your kids think about this question to themselves but not answer out loud: What would it take for you to totally surrender yourself to Jesus as Lord, obeying his every command, just like a character in a video game?

Conclude your session by saying something like this: Let's be willing to hand over the controller of our life to the Messiah. Let's choose to know him, obey him, and live like he is Lord.

Let your kids know you'll be sending them **5 for 5 world tour** life application and devotional challenges for them to do each day via Twitter, e-mail, or through a Facebook group you've set up. (Or, if you prefer not to use these technology options, pass out copies of the **5 for 5 world tour** handout you've downloaded from the CD-ROM to the teens.) Encourage your kids to strive to spend about 5 minutes each day connecting with God through these devotional experiences. ❤️

aftr u meet

Right after your meeting, send kids the first **5 for 5 world tour** challenge for them to do tomorrow via Twitter, e-mail, or by posting it on a Facebook page (or youth group Web page) you've set up. Continue to send 1 challenge each day for the 5 days following your meeting.

Prompt them to keep at it with their **5 for 5 world tour** challenges and let them know you're praying for them.

5 for 5 world tour

The Messiah
as Savior

The Prep

Session goal: Jr. highers will consider what "Jesus saves" truly means.

Scriptures: Luke 2:8-20; Luke 2:21-35; Luke 7:36-50; Luke 19:1-10

You'll need:

- Bibles
- Pens or pencils
- Slips of paper (2 or 3 per teen)
- 1 nativity scene
- World map
- 1 or more junk-mail fake credit cards or a credit card ad
- 1 pair of scissors
- 1 coin or other valuable object

Download and print:

- "Savior Symbols" handout (1 copy, cut apart)
- **solo/strike a chord** discussion guide (1 per teen)

Optional supplies:

✤ For **hit the road**: iPod or CD player and CD with recommended **playlist** music.

✤ For **hit the road**: Download and print copies of this week's **5 for 5 world tour** take-home page (1 per teen) if you are unable to use the technology options.

Setting it up:

✤ For **mic check**, select several odd English words from the dictionary or use the ones from the margin of the **mic check** section. Write each word and definition on a slip of paper.

✤ Have a nativity scene available but not set up for **strike a chord**.

✤ For **freestyle**, have 2 places in the room in mind for your teens to break into 2 discussion groups. In one area, place the world map and the "All the Earth" half of the "Savior Symbols" handout. In the other area, hide the valuable object (the coin or other item) for the kids to find. (Make sure it's hidden but won't take too much time to find.) And also place the "A Lost Object" half of the "Savior Symbols" handout in the area and write what object they will be searching for on it.

✤ If you're using the **playlist** recommendations, download one or all of the songs "Let God Arise" by Chris Tomlin, "Salvation is Here" by Lincoln Brewster, and "Salvation" from Passion (or Chris Tomlin) and ready your iPod or burn a CD in order to play the songs during the session.

Leader insight: ———

A side from various obnoxious or obscene words, the phrase "Jesus saves" may be one of the most commonly graffitied phrases on bridges, alleys, and bathroom stalls across America. Street preachers, billboards, and bumper stickers proclaim it. But what in the world does it actually mean?

To many, the phrase "Jesus saves" is basically about one thing: avoiding Hell and getting into Heaven.

Scripture provides us a much more rich, nuanced, and full picture of what it means to call Jesus the Savior. And this theme of salvation rings throughout Luke's Gospel like a clear, echoing bell. Over and over again, in various settings and conversations and events, we see salvation described in unique and surprising ways.

Luke begins with 2 people who spoke about the saving nature of Jesus' mission before he even came onto the scene. Zechariah, the father of John the Baptist, was the first to hear the news that the Messiah was coming and that his own miraculously conceived son would be the Messiah's forerunner. When John was born, Zechariah praised God, repeatedly talking about the coming salvation. In Luke 1:69, 71 Zechariah referenced salvation coming from the house of David and spoke of the salvation from enemies that a kingly Messiah would bring. Then in 1:77 he spoke of his son John's mission that complemented Jesus' mission, linking salvation directly with the forgiveness of sins. The second person mentioning Jesus' mission is Mary, Jesus' mother, who sang a song of praise as she was pregnant with Jesus. In her song, she called God "my Savior" (1:47).

When Jesus was actually born, the angel dramatically announced him as the "Savior" (Luke 2:11). Beyond all the other things that the angel could have first said about Jesus—he's the great High Priest, the King, the Son of God—the primary description the angel used was *Savior*.

Consider the significance of this: Before Jesus ever healed or taught or suffered or died or rose again, he was described at the Savior. Why? Because salvation was at the very core of the Messiah's mission on earth.

These are just the accounts of Jesus' infancy! As we read about the adult Jesus interacting with others, we begin to develop a full view of the salvation Jesus offers. It's much more than a ticket to Heaven! Perhaps one of the most significant descriptions of this salvation mission is one Jesus publicly claimed about himself in Luke 4:18-20: Jesus read from Isaiah 61 and declared himself to be the fulfillment of this messianic promise. He described salvation as freedom from bondage, oppression, and poverty. His salvation brought sight for the blind. In Jesus' lifetime, we see that he offered these things *literally*— he interacted with outcasts, he loved the poor, he healed the blind. His salvation partly had to do with life in *this* world—finding hope, peace, happiness, purpose, and deep satisfaction in this human life. Jesus' salvation also offers us these things *spiritually*—we are set free from the bondage of guilt, our spiritual poverty is assuaged, and we are offered eternal life.

So what about you? How full and deep and complete is your understanding of what it means to call Jesus your Savior? What does God want to teach you as you lead your kids through this exploration of Luke?

In preparation for leading this small group session, pray: Jesus, you are my Savior. You've saved me from sin and guilt and Hell. You've saved me from purposelessness, hopelessness, and bondage to a meaningless way of life. You've saved me into your presence and into joy, satisfaction, truth, and hope. Please help me communicate these truths with passion to my kids—and help each of them as they come to see the salvation you offer in a new and fresh way. In your name, Jesus the Savior, amen.

The Session

Rearrange or delete sections of the study to best meet your group's needs.

b4 u meet

A couple of days before your group meets, send a text message to your kids reminding them of the upcoming Pursue study. (If some teens don't text, send them an e-mail or a message on Facebook or MySpace.)

txt a frnd `about 2 minutes`

Invite your small group to consider this question:

★ Think of a time when someone misunderstood you. (Maybe a teacher thought you said one thing, but you said another. Maybe a friend thought a Facebook message was mean when you were really joking.) What happened? How did you fix the misunderstanding?

When they've got an answer, invite them to get out their cell phones and text their answer to another person in the room. (If kids don't have their own phone, they could borrow a friend's or could form pairs and talk about their answer to this question.)

When you're ready to move on to the next part of the study, have them put their cell phones away for now. ★

mic check `about 5-8 minutes`

Give each teen 2-3 slips of paper and pens or pencils. Explain how this game works. You'll read (and also spell out) a weird word from the English language and will also tell everybody what part of speech it is (noun, verb, etc.).

Each teen needs to write down that word and then create a fake definition for it. (Your kids may work in pairs if they prefer.) Their goal is to craft a definition that others will think is the *real* one.

solo/strike a chord handout

You'll collect the definitions from each teen or pair of teens and will also shuffle in the real definition you wrote out in advance. Next, read all the definitions aloud (with a straight face). The group should vote on which definition they believe is the correct one from the dictionary. Reveal which definition was the real one—and congratulate any teen who was able to successfully fool others with a fake definition.

As time allows, play several rounds of this game. When you're done, invite the group to share their ideas about which fake definition was the best. Then transition to the next activity by saying you are going to look at a word that may seem familiar at first but one that many people don't truly understand. 🏵

strike a chord   about 7-10 minutes

Say something like this to your group: **We've probably all heard that Jesus saves or he is our Savior. But what does that actually mean?**

Have your kids come up with a few definitions of "save" or "savior." Tell your kids that, according to thesaurus.com, synonyms for *savior* are: defender, deliverer, guardian, hero, liberator, preserver, protector, rescuer.

Let them know that throughout this session you'll be exploring parts of Jesus' life from the book of Luke and determining what it really means that he is Savior.

Bring out the nativity scene you have, and have the group set it up.

Give each teen a copy of the **solo/strike a chord** handout and a pen or pencil. Use the bottom half of the page to guide your small group Bible exploration and discussion together as a group. Here's a copy of the **strike a chord** text for you to use to guide your discussion time:

Read Luke 2:8-20 together and talk about these questions:

✺ We've heard this story over and over each Christmas, but let's look at it again. Why does it matter that the very first thing the angels said about Jesus was that he is Savior?

✺ What do you think the shepherds thought when the angels called Jesus, the Christ (or Messiah), the Savior?

✺ Even before he taught or performed miracles or died on the cross, Jesus was called the Savior. From the moment of his birth, offering salvation to humankind was at the very core of Jesus' mission on earth. What's your reaction to this idea? Why is it important?

Make sure to reiterate that salvation was at the core of Jesus' mission on earth, and it was made known from the beginning. ✺

txt it

If you want, invite kids to answer these questions both by talking aloud and by texting. As some share their answers, others can text them to you. Read some of their thoughts aloud and build upon their ideas as your group explores this topic together.

hidden track

Contrary to what some people may think, "Christ" is not Jesus' last name! You may want to remind the group that the word *Christ* is the New Testament version of the Hebrew word *Messiah*. Whenever Luke or other New Testament writers call Jesus the Christ, they are directly naming him as the Messiah.

Savior Symbols

freestyle `about 15-20 minutes`

Divide your teens into 2 groups. Take the 2 parts of the "Savior Symbols" handout and give one half to each group. Send the "A Lost Object" group to the part of the room where you hid the coin or other object. Then give the world map to the "All the Earth" group and send them to another part of the room. Have the groups work for about 10 minutes on the questions from their sheets. When there is about 2 minutes left of the 10, make sure they've gotten to the "Your Job" section that explains they will teach what they've just learned to the other group.

The "A Lost Object" group will look at the map and read Simeon's pronouncement about the baby Jesus in Luke 2:21-35. The key idea they'll explore is that through Jesus, salvation is offered to all the people of the earth, not just the Jews.

The "All the Earth" group will look for the object you hid. They'll read about Jesus' encounter with Zacchaeus in Luke 19:1-10 and Jesus' declaration that he came to save the lost. The key idea they'll explore is that salvation is for the lost; *anyone* (no matter how "bad") can be saved.

When the time is up, have the 2 groups come back together and take a minute or 2 each to teach the others the things they discussed from their passage. Make sure each group has communicated the key idea listed above or else you may want to reiterate. ✹

solo `about 5 minutes`

Tell your jr. highers you'd like them to find a spot in your meeting area where they can be alone and spend about 5 minutes reading Scripture and thinking about what it means.

Have your teens now work through the top half of the **solo/strike a chord** handout. Here's a copy of what they'll read:

Take 5 minutes to read Luke 7:36-50. Consider:
❋ What's the point of Jesus' story?
❋ How does this make you feel?

When the kids understand what they're supposed to do, have them take off and find a spot to read and reflect. After about 5 minutes, call everybody back together. ❋

encore `about 5 minutes`

Read Luke 7:36-50 together. Then discuss:
❋ How did the sinful woman treat Jesus? How did Jesus treat her?
❋ What's the point of Jesus' story? How would you explain his main point in your own words?
❋ Look again at 7:48-50. Jesus uses the word saved here. In light of the all that's happened in this account, what do you think Jesus means when he says she's been saved? What does this story tell you about salvation? ❋

txt it

If you want, invite kids to answer these questions both by talking aloud and by texting. As some share their answers, others can text them to you. Read some of their thoughts aloud and build upon their ideas as your group explores this topic together.

backstage pass `about 3 minutes`

Help your teens apply what Luke 7:36-50 and today's message of the Messiah as Savior means to their lives. Go over these points:

✦ In this passage, Jesus told a story about debts being cancelled. In his story, Jesus talks about *denarii*—an amount of money in his day. One denarius was about equivalent to what an average laborer or soldier would earn for an entire day's work. So, in Jesus' story, one man owed 50 denarii (which was about 50 day's wages) while the other owed 500 denarii—nearly 2 years' worth of wages!

✦ In our culture, there's no greater symbol of debt than credit cards. In fact, some statistics say that the average American family carries $8,000 in credit card debt.

Bring out the fake credit cards and/or credit card ads and the scissors. Pass them around to the teens and have each person make a cut. As they do, say something like this:

> Jesus came to earth to save us from our sin—the biggest debt we will ever have. Just as it would be a relief for someone to come along and pay monetary debts for us, we have much more peace spiritually now that Jesus has cancelled our sin debt with his salvation. ✦

playlist

As you end your small group time, play some upbeat worship songs focused on salvation to set an energizing tone as kids head out. Download one or all of the following songs to your iPod (or burn to a CD):
"Let God Arise" by Chris Tomlin
"Salvation is Here" by Lincoln Brewster
"Salvation" from Passion (or Chris Tomlin)

hit the road `about 2 minutes`

Summarize the key ideas you have discussed today about the Messiah as Savior. Gather all of the symbols you have used throughout the session. Hold each up and remind your group of their meaning:

- Nativity scene: From the very beginning of his life, salvation was at the core of Jesus' mission on earth.
- World map: Through Jesus, salvation is offered to all the people of the earth.
- Lost object: Jesus' salvation is for all the lost, no matter how "bad" we are.
- Cut up credit card: At its core, Jesus' salvation is about the forgiveness of our biggest debt—sin.

Wrap up with a time of prayer. If you have any kids who have never made a commitment to Jesus, be sure to let everyone know that you are available at any time to talk more about what it means to make Jesus the Lord and Savior of their lives.

Let your kids know you'll be sending them **5 for 5 world tour** life application and devotional challenges for them to do each day via Twitter, e-mail, or through a Facebook group you've set up. (Or, if you prefer not to use these technology options, pass out copies of the **5 for 5 world tour** handout you've downloaded from the CD-ROM to the teens.) Encourage your kids to strive to spend about 5 minutes each day connecting with God through these devotional experiences.

aftr u meet

Right after your meeting, send kids the first **5 for 5 world tour** challenge for them to do tomorrow via Twitter, e-mail, or by posting it on a Facebook page (or youth group Web page) you've set up. Continue to send 1 challenge each day for the 5 days following your meeting.

Prompt them to keep at it with their **5 for 5 world tour** challenges and let them know you're praying for them.

5 for 5 world tour

5 for 5 world tour
session 6

Set aside 5 minutes a day for the next 5 days to pursue God.

Day 1
Light a candle in your house. In Luke 2:32 Simeon calls Jesus "a light for revealed God." Look at the flame. How has Jesus revealed God to you?

Day 2
Ask a Christian older than you, "Can you tell me your story of finding Jesus' salvation? What difference has it made to you?" Then listen.

Day 3
If someone asked you, "What's your salvation story?" what would you say? Write how close saved you from? What has he brought into your life?

Day 4
You've thought about your salvation story. Now practice it and live it. Pray that way day you'll share it with a friend who needs to hear it.

Day 5
Jesus offers salvation to everyone. Who do you think would most follow Jesus? Pray for them. Ask Jesus to give you his love for them.

pursue · Session 6

7

The Messiah
as Life

The Prep

Session goal: Jr. highers will be challenged to find their ultimate satisfaction, rest, and contentment—true life!—in Jesus

Scriptures: John 1:1-5; John 3:16; John 4:4-15; John 5:24; John 6:25-40; John 8:12; John 10:10; John 11:25; John 14:6; John 17

You'll need:

- Bibles
- Pens or pencils
- Piece of paper
- 4 pitchers or containers to hold water
- 4 different kinds of water (see Setting It Up instructions)
- Cups (1 per teen)
- Roll paper
- Art supplies: colored pencils, markers, or crayons
- Bread (enough for a small piece/bite per teen)

Download and print:

- "Life Is" handout (1 per teen)
- **solo/strike a chord** discussion guide (1 per teen)

s:

ge pass: iPod or CD player and CD with
st music.

wnload and print copies of this week's 5 **for 5**
me page (1 per teen) if you are unable to use the
ns.

agazines, scissors, glue.

it up:

heck: Choose 4 different types of water. You might use
r, filtered water, or any brands of bottled water from the
Pour each kind of water into a different pitcher, and label the
ers 1, 2, 3, 4. (Make sure you keep track of which is which for
rself!) Set the water and cups for each teen and a piece of paper
d pen (for voting!) all together.

For **backstage pass:** Have bread available so each kid can break off
a piece. Also keep the water leftover from mic check (or get some
more) and have kids hold onto their cups so that everybody has a
sip or 2 to drink during this time.

✦ If you're using the **playlist** recommendations, download the songs
"Welcome to Your Life" by Me in Motion, "Come Alive" by Barlow-
Girl, "I'll Show You How to Live" by Sanctus Real, and "Hungry
(Falling On My Knees)" by Joy Williams and ready your iPod or
burn a CD in order to play the songs during the session.

Leader insight:

John's introduction of Jesus in his Gospel account may be one of the most intriguing and dynamic of any introduction of a single figure in literature. Standing apart from his historical narrative, John's first 18 verses present a figure so grand that it's difficult to ignore the implications.

It's interesting that John does not actually use the name *Jesus* until the seventeenth verse. Up to that point, John describes him as the Word (John 1:1), God (1:1), Creator (1:3), source of life (1:4), light (1:5, 9), and the prophesied Messiah (1:15). As if the opening 18 verses weren't intriguing enough, John concludes his prelude: "No one has ever seen God. But the unique One, who is himself God, is near to the Father's heart. He has revealed God to us" (1:18).

The rest of John's Gospel account certainly delivers. Jesus identified himself as the "living water" (John 4:10), "living bread" (6:51), and "light that leads to life" (8:12). The repetition of the word "life" in the Gospel suggests much more than mere biological existence. Jesus was talking about *living* and *life* as spiritual vitality, a rightness that leads to completeness. In 10:10 he stated, "My purpose is to give them a rich and satisfying life." John's claim to his Greek audience that's woven throughout his Gospel is simply this: True satisfaction, rest, contentment, and joy only come through the person of Jesus Christ.

To truly live as we were *meant* to live can only happen through the person and work of the Messiah. As a sort of concluding thesis, John wrote in John 20:31, "But these are written so that you may continue to believe that Jesus is the Messiah, the Son of God, and that by believing in him you will have life by the power of his name."

It is also interesting that John's Gospel places an especially strong emphasis on obedience. In the chapters that cover the intimate evening before Jesus' arrest (a significantly longer record of that night than in the other Gospels), Jesus told his disciples, "When you obey my commandments, you remain in my love, just as I obey my Father's commandments and remain in his love. I have told you these things so that you will be filled with my joy. Yes, your joy will overflow!" (John 15:10, 11).

In John's Gospel we learn that true living comes through Christ. But not only that: Joy comes only through a commitment and continued *obedience* to Jesus as the Messiah. Though it's certainly true that John's message was relevant to his original audience, it is quite remarkable that his message seems to grow in importance through history and is extremely relevant today in our contemporary culture driven by acquisition and consumption. People in our culture seem so preoccupied with finding happiness and avoiding suffering and discomfort—yet they are looking in all the wrong places for true satisfaction.

What about you? Is Jesus your source of true life? Do you seek the abundant life he offers, or do you settle for the superficial, self-centered lifestyle of our culture? How can you more deeply drink of the living water in your own everyday life?

In preparation for leading this small group session, pray: Lord Jesus, you are the author of life. Help me to find rest in your love by obeying your commands. Give me the strength to seek you above all other distractions of life. In the name of Jesus. Amen. ✹

The Session

Rearrange or delete sections of the study to best meet your group's needs.

b4 u meet

A couple of days before your group meets, send a text message to your kids reminding them of the upcoming Pursue study. (If some teens don't text, send them an e-mail or a message on Facebook or MySpace.)

txt a frnd about 2 minutes

Invite your small group to consider this question:

✤ If you had to eat at one restaurant every day for the rest of your life, what would it be?

When they've got an answer, invite them to get out their cell phones and text their answer to another person in the room. (If kids don't have their own phone, they could borrow a friend's or could form pairs and talk about their answer to this question.)

When you're ready to move on to the next part of the study, have them put their cell phones away for now. ✤

mic check about 3 minutes

Tell everybody you want help doing a taste test. Point out the table you set up with cups for everyone and the 4 different pitchers labeled 1, 2, 3, 4 with different kinds of water in them. Have kids pour a sip or 2 from the different pitchers until they have tried them all. Then have them write their votes on the piece of paper.

Count the votes and have kids guess what kind of water was the winner. Then reveal each type of water and let them share their thoughts or surprises on their tastes.

Transition by saying something like this: Today we are going to read about Jesus being described as a different kind of water: living

water. He's also described as *living* bread. Let's explore these ideas from the Gospel of John. ❧

strike a chord   about 10-12 minutes

Give each teen a copy of the **solo/strike a chord** handout and a pen or pencil. Use the bottom half of the page to guide your small group Bible exploration and discussion together as a group. Here's a copy of the **strike a chord** text for you to use to guide your discussion time:

Read John 4:4-15 together and talk about these questions:

❧ When Jesus offered the woman "living water," what do you think she was thinking?

❧ What do you think he really meant?

In the next story, Jesus had just miraculously multiplied bread and fish to feed a crowd of over 5,000 people (John 6:1-15). Now read John 6:25-40 together. (Jesus calls himself the "bread of life" again in verse 48 and the "living bread" in verse 51.)

❧ Do you think the people understood what "bread of life" meant?

❧ What similarities do you see between this story and the woman at the well story?

❧ Why do you think Jesus chose bread and water as symbols of him?

Ask follow-up questions to really get your group to think about these metaphors and what they mean. Help them see that Jesus uses physical food to open up conversations about spiritual food. Help them see that, just as food and drink provide nutrients and sustenance, Jesus nourishes and sustains the hunger and thirst of our souls. ✹

solo about 5 minutes

Tell your jr. highers you'd like them to find a spot in your meeting area where they can be alone and spend about 5 minutes reading Scripture and thinking about what it means.

Have your teens now work through the top half of the **solo/strike a chord** handout. Here's a copy of what they'll read:

Take 5 minutes to read John 1:1-5. Consider:
✹ Who is the Word?
✹ How has the Word brought life (verse 4)?

When the kids understand what they're supposed to do, have them take off and find a spot to read and reflect. After about 5 minutes, call everybody back together. ✹

encore about 15 minutes

Have someone read John 1:4 aloud. Then say something like: This is the first use of the word life in the book of John. He uses that word throughout his Gospel. We just studied 2 other examples when Jesus said he was living water and the bread of life. Let's look at other examples of Jesus as life.

Give everyone a copy of the "Life Is" handout and have your group break into pairs or

txt it

If you want, invite kids to answer these questions both by talking aloud and by texting. As some share their answers, others can text them to you. Read some of their thoughts aloud and build upon their ideas as your group explores this topic together.

Life Is

txt it

You may want to give your teens the option of texting their answers to these questions to you during your discussion time. Read some of their answers out loud and use them as springboards for further discussion.

groups of 3. Tell them to follow the instructions on their handout as they figure out what John means when he uses the word *zoe,* or "life."

Allow about 10 minutes for groups to work through their handouts. (Be sure to warn kids when they've got just a few minutes left, urging them to make sure they craft a definition together.) After 10 minutes, have everybody gather back together and invite a volunteer from each small group to share their group's definition of "life" (*zoe*).

✤ Use their definitions to facilitate a conversation on the significant passages they looked at.

✤ Ask them to explain their thoughts and talk about which specific verses most impacted their thoughts about the word *life*.

✤ Help draw out important aspects of life found in John, such as descriptions like eternal, spiritual, true, satisfying, wholeness, joy, and contentment.

Ask: What does it mean to have life in Jesus? ✤

freestyle   about 10-15 minutes

Allow your group to now express what they have learned about this concept of the Messiah being life. Put out the roll paper you brought and put out the art supplies for all to grab. Ask one kid to write the word LIFE in large, bold letters across the roll paper. Then have each kid grab some art supplies and draw pictures or write words that express the concepts of life you have studied to express the life Jesus brings to us all.

If you brought additional supplies, such as magazines, scissors, and glue, teens may have the option to cut out words or pictures to glue onto the LIFE project instead of (or in addition to) writing or drawing.

As teens work, casually look in on what they are creating and ask them to explain it to you or to the rest of the group. ✦

backstage pass   `about 5 minutes`

Use this time to allow your kids to thank God for the life he has given them through Jesus. Take the bread you brought and give a piece to each teen. Take the water you had leftover from **mic check** and pour a little into each teen's cup. This will be a time for your kids to commune with God, although it's not *exactly* communion!

Play the song listed in **playlist** (part 2) and ask your kids to spend these next 5 minutes in prayer, thinking about the life Jesus offers them. Encourage them to praise the Messiah for being life. Have them consider how he can make their lives even more satisfying when they give themselves over to him. As they pray, they can eat the bread and drink the water at anytime, considering how Jesus is living water and bread of life. ✦

hit the road   `about 1 minute`

Conclude by saying something like: The Messiah is Life. Though we have many wonderful things in life—family, friends, love, food,

playlist (part 1)

You might choose to play some upbeat music about life and living as followers of Jesus during this time. Download these songs to your iPod (or burn to a CD) and play them while kids create: "Welcome to Your Life" by Me in Motion "Come Alive" by BarlowGirl "I'll Show You How to Live" by Sanctus Real

playlist (part 2)

To add some prayerful ambiance about true hunger satisfied, download this song to your iPod (or burn to a CD) and play it while kids commune with God. "Hungry (Falling On My Knees)" by Joy Williams

aftr u meet

Right after your meeting, send kids the first 5 **for 5 world tour** challenge for them to do tomorrow via Twitter, e-mail, or by posting it on a Facebook page (or youth group Web page) you've set up. Continue to send 1 challenge each day for the 5 days following your meeting.

Prompt them to keep at it with their **5 for 5 world tour** challenges and let them know you're praying for them.

5 for 5 world tour

music, art, humor, beauty, and more—Jesus is the only true and lasting source of ultimate satisfaction and meaning. Make him your life.

Wrap up with a time of prayer.

Let your kids know you'll be sending them 5 **for 5 world tour** life application and devotional challenges for them to do each day via Twitter, e-mail, or through a Facebook group you've set up. (Or, if you prefer not to use these technology options, pass out copies of the 5 **for 5 world tour** handout you've downloaded from the CD-ROM to the teens.) Encourage your kids to strive to spend about 5 minutes each day connecting with God through these devotional experiences. ✦

The Messiah as Redeemer

The Prep

Session goal: Jr. highers will examine the implications of Jesus' death on the cross and will be challenged by God's call to live a new, redeemed life.

Scriptures: Romans 3:23-26; 2 Corinthians 5:16-18; Ephesians 4:22-24; Colossians 3:5-14

You'll need:

- Bibles
- Pens or pencils
- 1 ink pad (preferably red)
- Roll paper or a poster board
- Strips of fabric (1 per teen) that are a size and color for kids to write a word on them
- A few permanent or fabric markers

Download and print:

- "The T That's Me" handout (1 per teen)
- **solo/strike a chord** discussion guide (1 per teen)

Optional supplies:

- For **backstage pass** & **hit the road**: iPod or CD player and CD with recommended **playlist** music.
- For **hit the road**: Download and print copies of this week's **5 for 5 world tour** take-home page (1 per teen) if you are unable to use the technology options.
- For **mic check**: art supplies (either crayons or markers or colored pencils).
- For **freestyle**: 2 pieces of outerwear (such as hats, zip-up sweatshirts, jackets, etc.).

Setting it up:

- If you're doing the opening option for **freestyle**, put on a piece of outerwear (like a hat, jacket, or zip-up hoodie) before the study starts. Then have another one available to put on instead during the introduction of that activity.
- Also for **freestyle**, cut up strips of some type of fabric. (These will represent the clothes we are called to put on.) Make them large enough for your kids to write on (about 2 x 6 inches) and later use as bookmarks. Also have the permanent/fabric markers available for this activity.
- If you're using the **playlist** recommendation, download the song "Redeemer" by Nicole C. Mullen and ready your iPod or burn a CD in order to play it during the session.

Leader insight:

One of the greatest themes in Paul's writings is the transformed life of the believer. In 2 Corinthians 5:17, Paul declares, "anyone who belongs to Christ has become a new person." In Ephesians 4:22, 24, Paul says, "throw off your old sinful nature . . . put on your new nature." In Colossians 3:9, 10, he says, "you have stripped off your old sinful nature and all its wicked deeds. Put on your new nature, and be renewed as you learn to know your Creator and become like him."

In fact, it seems that all Paul's letters are cast in this general direction. Paul was continually concerned with believers realizing the fullness of their personhood, which is entirely based in who Christ is and what he has done on the cross. In short, it seems that Paul believed that Christians suffered from an identity crisis. Though the first church had been made new through Christ, they often still lived according to their old ways. This was a direct contradiction to the kingdom of God, to which they truly belonged. Even though the believers had accepted the sacrifice of Jesus and had been redeemed, Paul repeatedly lamented that their lives did not indicate this internal change.

This is tragic. Not only does this sort of inconsistency seem like betrayal, but the believer suffers because he does not experience the full life that is found in obedience to Christ's commands. This is the reason why Paul spent 11 chapters in Romans explaining the meaning of the cross and how it necessitates a response of holiness. Climatically, he wrote, "Don't copy the behavior and customs of this world, but let God transform you into a new person by changing the way you think" (Romans 12:2).

This idea of new life does not at all dismiss the complexity and difficulty of the continual struggle with sin that Christians face. Paul is simply saying that we belong to a strong, positive ethic of the kingdom—through the Trinitarian God, we no longer are characterized by, live according to, or are controlled by our sinful nature. Paul's adamant and persuasive argument is essential to living as a Christian.

Thus, redemption as a biblical theme has far reaching implications. Though it is based on the sacrifice of Jesus on the cross, it extends to every aspect of our being. Through Christ, our life has been made right. It is because of the cross and the continuing work of the Spirit that we are able to live a life worthy of the kingdom of God. We are meant to imitate God (Ephesians 5:1), and this is such a vital teaching in the church! Many people view church as a place of rules, hindering our freedom and our humanity. But Paul, along with the rest of Scripture, teaches it is only in obedience to Christ that we truly live.

So what about you? Are you living a redeemed life? Are you experiencing victory over sin and becoming more like Christ? Or do you feel trapped in a cycle of the "old life"? As you prepare to lead this study, take time on your own this week to honestly assess your own patterns of living. Invite God to work mightily in your life, renewing your vision for living a redeemed life.

In preparation for leading this small group session, pray: God, teach my kids (and teach me!) the joy of obedience. Help us gain inspiration from the cross and remind us of our new nature as redeemed people. Lord, let our lives align with your righteousness. In the name of the Redeemer, I pray. Amen. ✹

b4 u meet

A couple of days before your group meets, send a text message to your kids reminding them of the upcoming Pursue study. (If some teens don't text, send them an e-mail or a message on Facebook or MySpace.)

The Session

Rearrange or delete sections of the study to best meet your group's needs.

txt a frnd [about 2 minutes]

Invite your small group to consider this question:

✦**What's your favorite thing to wear?**

When they've got an answer, invite them to get out their cell phones and text their answer to another person in the room. (If kids don't have their own phone, they could borrow a friend's or could form pairs and talk about their answer to this question.)

When you're ready to move on to the next part of the study, have them put their cell phones away for now. ✦

mic check [about 5-7 minutes]

Give each teen a copy of "The T That's Me." If you brought crayons, markers, or colored pencils, allow your kids to access them. If not, they can use a pen or pencil. Instruct your teens to design their own T-shirts to express something about themselves. They can use words, pictures, whatever. Encourage them to think creatively and think of something they would really wear.

After some time, have everybody share their designs. Then transition by saying something

The T That's Me

"The T That's Me"

pursue · Session 8

like this: Today we're going to look at our response to the Messiah as Redeemer. We'll find out he has some things he wants us to wear. ✹

solo `about 5 minutes`

Tell your jr. highers you'd like them to find a spot in your meeting area where they can be alone and spend about 5 minutes reading Scripture and thinking about what it means.

Tell them that this Scripture passage will focus them on the redemption that Jesus offers us.

Give each teen a copy of the **solo/strike a chord** handout and a pen or pencil, inviting them to read and follow the instructions.

solo/strike a chord handout

(Have them read through only the top portion, **solo**, right now; they'll need the **strike a chord** portion in a few minutes.) Here's a copy of what they'll read:

Take 5 minutes to read Romans 3:23-26. Consider:
✹ How do you feel when you read this passage?
✹ Based on these verses, what is Jesus' redemption all about?

When the kids understand what they're supposed to do, have them take off and find a spot to read and reflect. After about 5 minutes, call everybody back together. ✹

strike a chord `about 10-15 minutes`

Have the group now look at the bottom portion of the **solo/strike a chord** handout and use it to guide your small group Bible explora-tion and discussion together as a group. Here's a copy of the **strike a**

txt it

If you want, invite kids to answer these questions both by talking aloud and by texting. As some share their answers, others can text them to you. Read some of their thoughts aloud and build upon their ideas as your group explores this topic together.

chord text for you to use to guide your discussion time:

Read Romans 3:23 together. Then consider:

✸ Look at your fingerprint. Every person's is unique. We are all different, yet we all share something in common—we sin. How does that make you feel?

Read Romans 3:24, 25 now. Then consider:

✸ Fortunately, we have another thing in common—we are all offered freedom from our sin. What is required of us to gain this freedom?

Read Romans 3:26 together. Then consider:

✸ This says God is "fair and just." Is it fair and just that Jesus, who lived a perfect life, died for all the rest of us who sin? ? ?

Give your kids time to wrestle with these deep questions. For the second question, remind them that we cannot "earn" Jesus' redemption, but we do take action by believing in him to receive such favor. For the third question, say that it doesn't seem fair—but our sins required blood, and Jesus offered that blood so that we (sinners) could have a relationship with God (holy).

Reiterate that Jesus, the Messiah, died a brutal death on the cross *for our sins*. He took the punishment we each deserved and has "bought" or "redeemed" our lives.

Now get out the red ink pad you brought and the poster board or roll paper. Have your kids ink their fingers and work together to each place fingerprints on the paper into the shape of one giant cross. Explain the idea that this is them identifying themselves with Jesus' death and the new life he offers. ✤

encore `about 15-20 minutes`

Begin this next segment of your study by emphasizing these ideas:

✤ Believing in the Messiah is more than just acknowledging the facts about his life—it is recognizing your part in his death and suffering. It is understanding what he did *for you* and what it means in your life.

✤ True belief in the Messiah, the Redeemer, means your life changes. Being a Christian in name only doesn't cut it; calling yourself a Christian isn't what it is all about. It means your whole identity is changed.

Lead the group through a study of 3 passages from Paul's epistles. Explain that Paul's original letters were read out loud to the Christian communities who received them. The church would gather and listen to Paul's words. Invite your kids to sit and listen carefully, receiving Paul's words like the Early Church first did: by hearing it.

Slowly and emphatically read 2 Corinthians 5:16-18 aloud. Afterward, invite kids to take a minute to write down their gut reaction to the passage on the back of their **solo/strike a chord** handout. After a moment of writing, invite kids to share their initial observations on the passage by asking: What did you think or feel as you heard that passage?

Now, tell the kids they'll hear the passage again, and this time they should write down any important or interesting words they hear in it. Read the passage aloud a second time. Then ask: What words stood out to you? (If they don't point it out, specifically mention "new person" and "new life" and "reconciling.")

✤ What do you think having a new life means? What does it mean that we need to reconcile others to God?

Next read Ephesians 4:22-24. Ask: Did you hear forms of the word new? Listen again, and figure out what needs to be renewed or be in your new

txt it

You may want to give your teens the option of texting their answers to these questions to you during your discussion time. Read some of their answers out loud and use them as springboards for further discussion.

nature. Read Ephesians 4:22-24 and have your teens write down and then tell you what those things are renewed or part of the new nature.

Finally, read Colossians 3:5-14 and have your kids follow along in their Bibles. Ask: Once Jesus has redeemed us, what things are we supposed to remove from our old way of life? What new things are we supposed to put on? ✸

freestyle `about 5 minutes`

As you say the following, if you can, take off one piece of outerwear (such as a hat, zip-up sweatshirt, jacket, etc.) and put a new piece on:

Paul described taking off our old actions and putting on the new self. How good does it feel to take off clothes once they get dirty and grimy? Putting on new clean clothes feels good. And that's the same feeling we should get as we respond to Jesus. Because Jesus died, we are no longer grimy and dirty. We have the chance to put on new clothes! And these clothes will identify us with Jesus.

Reread Colossians 3:12, 14: "Clothe yourselves with tenderhearted mercy, kindness, humility, gentleness, and patience . . . Above all, clothe yourselves with love."

Pass out one piece of fabric to each teen. Also make markers available. Ask your kids to write down at least one of the qualities above that they need to clothe themselves with. Or they may choose to write the Scripture reference or some other reminder of their response to Jesus' redemption.

Say: So dress appropriately—in other words, put on spiritual items that honor Jesus.

Have kids put their piece of fabric in their Bibles as a bookmark that can remind them of today's study. ✸

backstage pass & hit the road about 5 minutes

Have your kids get in small pairs or trios and ask them to take some time to pray for each other. Challenge them to specifically pray that the cross—and what Jesus did there to redeem them—would become more and more real to them. Allow a few minutes for them to pray, then you pray aloud for your jr. highers, asking God to continue to help them live a new life—a redeemed life of holiness and obedience.

Let your kids know you'll be sending them **5 for 5 world tour** life application and devotional challenges for them to do each day via Twitter, e-mail, or through a Facebook group you've set up. (Or, if you prefer not to use these technology options, pass out copies of the **5 for 5 world tour** handout you've downloaded from the CD-ROM to the teens.) Encourage your kids to strive to spend about 5 minutes each day connecting with God through these devotional experiences. ✦

aftr u meet

Right after your meeting, send kids the first **5 for 5 world tour** challenge for them to do tomorrow via Twitter, e-mail, or by posting it on a Facebook page (or youth group Web page) you've set up. Continue to send 1 challenge each day for the 5 days following your meeting.

Prompt them to keep at it with their **5 for 5 world tour** challenges and let them know you're praying for them.

playlist

To add some ambiance to this prayer time, download this song to your iPod (or burn to a CD) and play it while kids pray. Encourage them to listen to the words as well. "Redeemer" by Nicole C. Mullen

hidden track

If you have kids who have not made a faith commitment to Jesus, remind the group that they are welcome to talk with you personally about their questions or ideas. You may notice that specific kids didn't quite get what you've been saying about the redemption Jesus offers. If you feel a nudging by God's Spirit, seek out those teens during the week to talk further.

5 for 5 world tour

5 for 5 world tour
session 8

let some 5 minutes a day for the next 5 days to pursue God

Day 1
Create a five-word poem today about Jesus or your Redeemer.

Day 2
Where are you in your relationship with the Redeemer? What can you do you need to take to grow a new creation in Christ?

Day 3
Use a readable reader to splice a color generation on you. He'd about what it means to identify yourself with Jesus' death on the cross.

Day 4
Look around you today. Who needs to hear about Jesus' redemption? Pray that God would open doors for you to share his love with that person.

Day 5
Before you change actions today, read Colossians 2:13-14 again. What will you insert in a spiritual sense today?

purpose · Session 8

The Messiah as Lion and Lamb

The Prep

Session goal: Jr. highers will be challenged to eagerly await the coming of the Messiah as Lion and Lamb, ultimately fulfilling all God's promises.

Scriptures: Revelation 5:1-8

You'll need:

- Bibles
- Pens or pencils
- Prepared slips of paper
- 1 coin
- Markers
- Scissors
- Glue
- 1 piece of poster board or roll paper

Download and print:

- "Messiah: My Hope" handout (1 per teen)
- **solo/strike a chord** discussion guide (1 per teen)

Optional supplies:

- ✦ For **backstage pass:** iPod or CD player and CD with recommended **playlist** music.
- ✦ For **hit the road:** Download and print copies of this week's **5 for 5 world tour** take-home page (1 per teen) if you are unable to use the technology options.
- ✦ For **encore:** snacks.
- ✦ For **encore:** photomosaic examples online or printed out (see Setting It Up instructions).

Setting it up:

- ✦ For **mic check**, write the following animals on slips of paper, and place them in this order: pig, alligator, tiger, turtle, ostrich, anteater, donkey, hippo, koala bear, water buffalo.
- ✦ For **freestyle:** collect newspapers, news magazines, and/or print out top stories from the week's news from news Web sites like www.cnn.com. Set these in a pile and ready scissors, markers, and glue.
- ✦ Option for **encore:** a photomosaic is a large image that is made up of many small photos. You can view some on the site of their initial creator, Robert Silvers (www.photomosaic.com). Ready your computer to show a few of these to your group or print out 1 or 2.
- ✦ If you're using the **playlist** recommendations, download the songs "Chariot" by Page France and "Hail the Lord's Anointed" by The Welcome Wagon and ready your iPod or burn a CD in order to play the songs during the session.

Leader insight:

Contemporary Christian study of the book Revelation has often been rather dubious. Many times the book has been treated as solely a look into future events. It's been used by well-meaning and over-exuberant Christians to justify obsessions with trying to identify the antichrist, trying to read the signs of the times, and so on. When Christians approach the book in this manner, they end up missing out on its dynamic pastoral and literary quality. Fixating only on the prophetic nature of the book distracts from its real beauty and power. It's not merely prophetic—it's apocalyptic. The first word of the book is in fact *apokalypsis*, translated as "revelation" (Revelation 1:1). This demands that the book be read and understood as visual and symbolic literature.

But perhaps the most important key to understanding the purpose of the book is that we must view Revelation as a *letter*. John addresses it to "the seven churches in the province of Asia" (Revelation 1:4). In *New Testament Theology*, I. H. Marshall writes, "The purpose of the book is not primarily to satisfy curiosity about the detailed course of future events but rather to prepare and encourage a group of churches that were on the whole ill-equipped spiritually to face a future in which faith would be tried to the limit" (I. Howard Marshall, *New Testament Theology* [Downers Grove: Intervarsity Press, 2004], 548).

This angle certainly changes our engagement with the text! It means that ultimately the content of Revelation was meant not as "clues" to a big mystery, but rather to bolster the tenacity of believers under persecution and to instill in them a resolve of faith that would endure any trial. The original recipients of this letter were provided with a series of God-given "scenes" in order to displace their fear of the Roman emperor Domitian and his persecution of them. Instead,

Revelation urged them to have a right and proper fear of the vastly superior Messiah. Jesus is described as a powerful, awe-inspiring warrior in chapters 1 and 19. In the end of the book, the forces of evil are rendered pathetically inferior to the might of Jesus (see Revelation 19:19-21 and 20:10). In John's Gospel, Jesus rides into Jerusalem on a donkey; now in this epistle from John, Jesus rides in triumph on a white warhorse.

The descriptive, visual aspects of the book should be taken seriously. In fact, our emotional response to these scenes is integral to our sense of the meaning of the text. Not only do we encounter a picture of a majestic and awesome military King, but we witness his wrath and sovereignty in the 7 seals, the 7 trumpets, the 7 bowls, and all the other parenthetical visions. The details offered in these scenes work together to leave the audience with a lasting response of faithfulness and hope. In other words, the visual nature of the book has a certain way of convincing the reader of the truth it represents and leaves us with a lingering effect.

This brings us to one of the most fascinating details in the book and one of the most dramatic scenes in all of Scripture. In chapter 5, no one is found worthy to open the scroll. Revelation 5:5, 6 describes how the angel comforted John, saying, "Stop weeping! Look, the Lion of the tribe of Judah . . . is worthy to open the scroll." John then said, "Then I saw a Lamb." All the promises of the Messiah and all the hopes of the people come together in this scene; drawing upon the servant-king dichotomy of Isaiah, Revelation is an account of the victory of the Messiah as *both* the ferocious, powerful Lion and the sacrificial Lamb.

Surprisingly, from this point forward in Revelation, Jesus is not once directly referred to as the Lion again. However, he is called a Lamb in Revelation over 30 times. The point is clear: We are to assume that the Lion *is* the Lamb. Over and over again, through the image of the Lamb, Revelation reminds us that God has reconciled humanity unto himself and in the end will bring about the true fellowship with his creation that he always intended. This is in fact where the book of Revelation resolves: "They will see his face" (Revelation 22:4) and will be thirsty no more (22:17).

As you wrap up this series, invite God to speak to you in new and fresh ways through Revelation. Allow the descriptions of John's vision to enter into your imagination—step inside the scenes. Ask God to make the power and emotion of each scene bolster your own faith as it did the first recipients of this letter.

In preparation to lead this final small group session, pray: Lord Jesus, Messiah. You are the victorious Lion who will finally bring justice to our broken world. You will rule in truth and majesty. You are the sacrificial Lamb who took all the sin and brokenness of our world upon yourself on the cross. My hope is in you, Jesus, and in your eventual return to set things right in this world. Please help my kids develop this same hope in you—in both your majestic glory and your sacrificial love. In Jesus' name I pray, amen.

b4 u meet

A couple of days before your group meets, send a text message to your kids reminding them of the upcoming Pursue study. (If some teens don't text, send them an e-mail or a message on Facebook or MySpace.)

The Session

Rearrange or delete sections of the study to best meet your group's needs.

txt a frnd `about 2 minutes`

Invite your small group to consider this question:

✹ If you could be any animal, what would you be? Why?

   When they've got an answer, invite them to get out their cell phones and text their answer to another person in the room. (If kids don't have their own phone, they could borrow a friend's or could form pairs and talk about their answer to this question.)

   When you're ready to move on to the next part of the study, have them put their cell phones away for now. ✹

mic check `about 7-10 minutes`

Start off with a silly game before diving into this serious study. Divide into 2 teams. Explain that they're going to play speed charades. The game works this way:

✦ You'll hand a slip of paper to a person from one team. He or she then has *only 30 seconds* to act out what's written on that paper.

✦ Typical charades rules apply: The actor cannot talk, use props, or make any sounds.

✦ The teammates try to guess (while the other team watches silently). If they guess correctly in 30 seconds, they get 2 points. If they *don't* guess correctly, the opposite team members have one chance for a quick guess. If they get it right, they get 1 point.

* You then do the same with the other team and continue alternating their 30-second rounds.

* Let the group know that all of the slips are animals.

* Give teams these slips for the 5 rounds in this order: pig, alligator, tiger, turtle, ostrich, anteater, donkey, hippo, koala bear, water buffalo.

After you go through all the animal clues, appoint a winner. Then ask: Which animal best matches your personality? Why? Lead into the study by letting them know that Jesus was described as different animals. Today you're going to see him as Lion and Lamb. ✦

solo `about 5 minutes`

solo/strike a chord handout

Tell your jr. highers you'd like them to find a spot in your meeting area where they can be alone and spend about 5 minutes reading Scripture and thinking about what it means.

Tell them that this small group session will focus on the book of Revelation, specifically looking at Jesus as Lion and Lamb.

Give each teen a copy of the **solo/strike a chord** handout and a pen or pencil, inviting them to read and follow the instructions. (Have them read through only the top portion, **solo**, right now; they'll need the **strike a chord** portion in a few minutes.) Here's a copy of what they'll read:

Take 5 minutes to read Revelation 5:1-8. Consider:

* What images capture your attention the most in this passage?

* What emotions does this description of Jesus make you feel?

When the kids understand what they're supposed to do, have them take off and find a spot to read and reflect. After about 5 minutes, call everybody back together. ✹

strike a chord   about 10-15 minutes

solo/strike a chord handout

Have your kids turn to Revelation in their Bibles and provide some basic background about it.

✦ Revelation was written by John, Jesus' disciple who also wrote the Gospel of John and the epistles 1, 2, and 3 John.

✦ Revelation is a letter from John to 7 Christian communities. Christians were under severe persecution, and John's letter to them served as an encouragement.

✦ Revelation is imagery-based literature that works like visual media, like movies do for us today. If we read it properly, allowing John to build a world of sights and sounds in our minds, then it will help us grasp some important truths about the Messiah. When John wrote it, via the Holy Spirit, he didn't intend for his readers to try and analyze every detail in the book about the end times. Rather, it was to give them (and us!) a new way of looking at the world and a strengthening of faith.

Have the group now look at the bottom portion of the **solo/strike a chord** handout and use it to guide your small group Bible exploration and discussion together as a group. Here's a copy of the **strike a chord** text for you to use to guide your discussion time:

Reread Revelation 5:1-8 together. There are 6 main "characters" of this Scripture passage:
* God sitting on the throne
* 4 living creatures
* 24 elders
* John witnessing these visions
* An angel who helps John navigate these visions
* The Messiah figure who is the hero

Talk about these questions:
* What details do you notice in this scene that are surprising or memorable?
* Why do you think John wept?
* Why was the Lamb able to open the scroll when no one else could?

John is told, "Look, the Lion of the tribe of Judah" (Revelation 5:5), but when John looks, he doesn't see a Lion but rather a Lamb (verse 6). Ask:
* Why do you think the Lion turned into the Lamb?

Take some time to teach teens from this scene by touching on these key points:
* In this scene, the Lion and the Lamb are the same figure. Hold up a coin and briefly describe what is on each side. Make the point that it has 2 sides but is counted as just one coin. In fact, the images are meant to display 2 ideas about America and should be understood *together*. In a similar fashion,

hidden track

Though many immediately think about end-times prophecies when they hear the word *Revelation*, it is critical that you help your group constantly keep in mind this book's initial audience and their context. Continually prod your kids to think about how the early Christians would have received and understood the book. Their focus was on the encouragement of a victorious Messiah as they faced persecution.

txt it

If you want, invite kids to answer these questions both by talking aloud and by texting. As some share their answers, others can text them to you. Read some of their thoughts aloud and build upon their ideas as your group explores this topic together.

Jesus is presented as 2-sided in this scene. He is a Lion: powerful, mighty, and ferocious. He is a Lamb: meek, peaceful, a creature killed in sacrifice for sins.

✦ These 2 images encompass the 2 largest aspects of the Messiah woven throughout the Bible. The powerful, ruling Lion reminds us that the Messiah is the King, the Son of God, and the Lord of all. The Lamb reminds us that the Messiah is the Priest who sacrificed himself. He's a suffering Servant. He's the Savior. He's Life. He's Redeemer. ✦

freestyle `about 10 minutes`

Begin by saying something like this: The early Christians who received John's letter of Revelation lived in a dark time. We also live in a world of pain, suffering, and sin.

Invite each teen to grab a newspaper, magazine, or a handful of printouts from the Internet that you've made available. Give everybody some scissors. Direct kids to take about 3 minutes to look through the stories and each cut out 1 or 2 bad news stories—news that captures the brokenness, violence, injustice, depravity, or heartache of this world. Then each teen should cut out a square or 2 from the story.

Next, say something like: In Revelation, we also see the final victory of the Messiah and the fulfillment of all God's promises. Like the people of the Bible, from Old Testament to New, we are also waiting in hope for the time when the Messiah will rule and be the solution to all our earthly pain.

Explain that the Messiah is the most relevant answer to all of the problems in our world. As the Lion, he is the ruling King who will bring justice and peace. As the sacrificial Lamb, he brings forgiveness, spiritual wholeness, and satisfaction of our deepest yearnings.

Challenge pairs to look at the stories and headlines they've cut out and decide which aspect of the Messiah will ultimately answer that problem, then have them use a marker to write either "LION" or "LAMB" in large print atop their story or headline based on what the story is about. (For example, a story about murder would be best answered by the Lion who will one day bring justice and victory over violence and evil. A story about suicide might be best answered by the Lamb who offers spiritual wholeness and satisfaction of our deepest needs.)

Once pairs have labeled their stories, have them gather around the poster or paper and glue the stories to the appropriate section: the Lion section or the Lamb section. They should create a LION collage on half the paper and a LAMB collage on the other half. As they do, they can discuss their stories with others if they'd like to.

End by saying something like this: Until Jesus returns, our world will be full of problems and heartache. But we have an amazing hope: Our Messiah is the Lion and the Lamb who will eventually make everything right. ✦

backstage pass   about 8 minutes

Pass out the "Messiah: My Hope" handouts and pens. Then direct kids to spread out around the room and find their own space to sit and reflect. Explain that you'd like them to use the handout to guide a time of reflection on all they've learned about the Messiah over the past 9 weeks. Encourage them to take the next several minutes to meet with God—to pray silently, to write their prayers, to draw images in prayer, or to just listen to the lyrics

Messiah: My Hope

playlist

The songs below both use indie-folk music and a poetic style to describe the hope that is only fulfilled in Jesus and in his return at the end of time. Download them to your iPod or burn a CD and play them to set a reflective tone for kids during this concluding section of the study:
"Chariot" by Page France
"Hail the Lord's Anointed" by The Welcome Wagon

txt it

If you want, invite kids to answer these questions both by talking aloud and by texting. As some share their answers, others can text them to you. Read some of their thoughts aloud and build upon their ideas as your group explores this topic together.

of the songs you'll play (if you are using the **playlist** suggestions). ✦

encore   `about 5 minutes`

Take some time to celebrate what your group has done and learned over the past 9 studies. If you brought snacks, invite your kids to grab some and sit back for a few minutes to debrief together.

Show them the samples of photomosaics that you prepared. Explain that a photomosaic is a collection of small photos that, when put together, allow us to step back and see a big picture too.

Compare this study series on the Messiah to a photomosaic: You've looked at 9 different images of the Messiah, but they all go together to create a big picture of who he is. Repeat the 9 images: High Priest, King, Servant, Son of God, Lord, Savior, Life, Redeemer, Lion and Lamb.

Lead the group in a relaxed discussion of the questions they considered in the **backstage pass** activity:

✦ How did this study series change the way you think about Jesus?

✦ Which image of the Messiah challenged you the most? Which surprised you the most? Why?

✦ Think back to where you were in your relationship with God and in your spiritual journey before you started this small group series. How has God changed you through your exploration of the Messiah?

Congratulate your group's insights and growth through this time together. ✦

hit the road `about 1-2 minutes`

Close out this session and entire study with a time of prayer. You may choose to have your kids pray for one another or you may want to pray only. You might close with something like this:

Jesus, our Messiah, you are so much more than we can fully understand or imagine. Thank you for loving us so much that you died and rose again for us. Thank you for being approachable yet holy. Thank you for being the answer to all of our problems and the satisfaction to all our needs. Help us to know you more, to love you more, and to live for you more each day. In your name, Jesus, we pray. Amen.

Let your kids know you'll be sending them **5 for 5 world tour** life application and devotional challenges for them to do each day via Twitter, e-mail, or through a Facebook group you've set up. (Or, if you prefer not to use these technology options, pass out copies of the **5 for 5 world tour** handout you've downloaded from the CD-ROM to the teens.) Encourage your kids to strive to spend about 5 minutes each day connecting with God through these devotional experiences. ✦

5 for 5 world tour

aftr u meet

Right after your meeting, send kids the first **5 for 5 world tour** challenge for them to do tomorrow via Twitter, e-mail, or by posting it on a Facebook page (or youth group Web page) you've set up. Continue to send 1 challenge each day for the 5 days following your meeting.

Prompt them to keep at it with their **5 for 5 world tour** challenges and let them know you're praying for them.

Scripture index